ENVIRONMENTAL   SCIENCE   TECHNOLOGY

INFORMATION   RESOURCES

ENVIRONMENTAL SCIENCE TECHNOLOGY

INFORMATION RESOURCES

Edited by Dr. Sidney B. Tuwiner in
conjunction with the Chemical International
Information Center (Chemists' Club)

NOYES DATA CORPORATION

Park Ridge, New Jersey   London, England
1973

Copyright © 1973 by Chemical International Information Center (The Chemists' Club)
No part of this book may be reproduced in any form
without permission in writing from the Publisher.
Library of Congress Catalog Card Number: 72-90900
ISBN: 0-8155-0467-5
Printed in the United States

Published in the United States of America
by Noyes Data Corporation
Noyes Building, Park Ridge, New Jersey 07656

FOREWORD

This book is a direct result of the rapidly increasing demand for methods by which environmental information may be obtained. Realizing this demand, the Chemical International Information Center, at the Chemists' Club, New York, held a Symposium to bring together interested professionals and authorities in environmental information retrieval. In order to make this book more valuable, the CIIC furnished additional material from the Environmental Protection Agency and the United Nations, to be included in this book.

Section I includes the proceedings and panel discussion of the Symposium on Environmental Science Technology Information Resources sponsored by the Chemical International Information Center, and held at the Chemists' Club, New York, N.Y., on April 28, 1972.

Section II includes selected papers presented at the National Environmental Information Symposium, sponsored by the EPA, held at Cincinnati, Ohio, September 24-27, 1972.

Section III is a bibliography of basic governmental, institutional and organizational documents assembled by the United Nations Conference on the Human Environment, held at Stockholm, Sweden, June 5-16, 1972.

Environmental science is a new science in many of its aspects. Being a subject of high actuality, it has led to a proliferation of many new publications, stemming from a pressing need for continual updating of the technology and its literature, codes regulating discharges and emissions, etc.

Environmental science is interdisciplinary, involving sociology, law and economics, as well as technology. Some of the problems arising from this fact are discussed here and solutions are attempted.

The individual papers give a close look at the many sources of environmental information from the several viewpoints of librarian, editor and specialist in government sources or industry associations, enabling the user to obtain a broad perspective on environmental information.

The Chemical International Information Center (Chemists' Club) wishes to thank the Environmental Protection Agency and the United Nations for granting permission to publish Sections II and III.

CONTENTS

SECTION I

Introductory Remarks   2
    Sidney B. Tuwiner, Ph.D.

Resources and Industrial Cooperation on Environmental Control at the American
Petroleum Institute   9
    E.H. Brenner

Environmental Protection Agency and Its R&D Program   15
    William J. Lacy

Government Sources of Information on Environmental Control   25
    Marshall Sittig

Sorting It Out – Data vs. Information   35
    Steven S. Ross

Environmental Control Resources of a Large Technical Library   52
    Kirk Cabeen

Panel Discussion   57
    Sidney B. Tuwiner, Ph.D.

SECTION II

Technical Information Programs in the Environmental Protection Agency   68
    A.C. Trakowski

EDS Environmental Science Information Center   78
    James. E. Caskey

Federal Environmental Data Centers and Systems   82
    Arnold R. Hull

Scientific and Technical Information Centers Concerned with the Biological
Sciences   89
    William B. Cottrell

Scientific and Technical Primary Publications Carrying Environmental
Information   107
    D.H. Michael Bowen

Secondary Technical and Scientific Journals   119
    Bernard D. Rosenthal

Environmental Litigation as a Source of Environmental Information   124
    Victor J. Yannacone, Jr.

Applications of Socioeconomic Information to Environmental Research and
Planning   128
    William B. DeVille

Socioeconomic Aspects of Environmental Problems – Secondary Information
Sources   134
    James G. Kollegger

Selected Listing of Information Centers and Services Available in the
Socioeconomic Area   157

SECTION III

Introduction   172

Basic Documents Received from States Invited to the Conference   175

Basic Documents Prepared Within the United Nations System   191

Basic Documents Received from Other Sources   203

Draft Position Papers   216

Other Papers   218

SECTION I

Proceedings and Panel Discussion of the Symposium on Environmental Science and Technology Information Resources, sponsored by the Chemical International Information Center, and held at the Chemists' Club, New York, N.Y., on April 28, 1972.

INTRODUCTORY REMARKS

Sidney B. Tuwiner, Ph.D.
Professional Engineer
New York, New York

To all of you who have come to participate in this annual symposium of the Chemists' Club Library I would like to address, at the beginning, a word of thanks on behalf of the Committee, the Library and the Club. It is you who have made it possible for us to conduct this event annually and it is now quite well established as a tradition which we are striving mightily to continue and expand.

Each year we have selected a subject within the broad umbrella of information science which is both topical and important to you who attend these events. We would be pleased to receive your comments as well as suggestions for future symposia. This year we have selected the topic of environmental information. In some of its aspects environmental science is new. It has, at any rate, led to a proliferation of many new publications and, furthermore, it has resulted in a need for continued updating of technology, codes regulating discharges and emissions, standards for air and water, etc.

Environmental science is interdisciplinary, involving sociology, law and economics as well as technology. This presents what some like to call challenges. I prefer to call them problems. A problem becomes a challenge only in retrospect after it has been solved.

Information, like gold, is where you find it. This means that it may sometimes be necessary to improvise and blaze an occasional new trail to sources which are normally entirely outside of the field of interest of information researches. One of our purposes in presenting this symposium is to point out some of these nonclassical sources and the means for reaching them. My own very limited contribution to this is to present the view of a client who is served by information specialists and one who has had perforce to serve himself in acquiring or retrieving environmental information. I want to share some of my experiences with you in the hope that these may shed some light on the problems which we all run into from time to time.

I am very candid in confessing that these examples are ones which you who are here today will, in all probability, never encounter in a lifetime. They are intended only as illustrations of a philosophy of approach. Firstly, I am unwilling to accept that any information or data is entirely lacking for any given problem. Secondly, I am unwilling to accept that anything, other than that relating to death and taxes, is known with perfect certainty. In real life we design systems and exercise judgement on the basis of reasonableness and probability.

For example, if we are seeking the properties of a substance and we find, after exhaustive research, that the specific data is unavailable, we next look for the corresponding data for homologues, analogues and isomers. We then extrapolate or interpolate and thus arrive at the most probable estimate. We also take care to estimate the degree of reliability of our estimate. On the other hand if we find the data we are seeking in a table in some handbook we should be wary of accepting it without reference to the original source and an estimate of its precision and reliability.

The same considerations apply to system performance parameters, economic and market information, toxicological data, environmental impact evaluation, etc., etc. Retrieval of information implies evaluation without which there has been no exercise of professional skill.

This is not to imply that every request for information justifies the full treatment of search and evaluation. After all we have the problem, recently brought sharply into focus, that our resources for information research are not limitless. We must therefore budget our time and effort to optimize the fulfillment of our requirements. In order to do this effectively it is necessary for the technical person and the information person to communicate. It is the most stupid, yet most commonplace practice for someone to request all of the information pertaining to a subject without setting some limit upon the effort which is justified.

It is for this reason that corporate management often imposes an interdepartmental transfer in the financial accounts and then subjects the departments to budgetary controls. This practice is far from ideal inasmuch as it imposes additional requirements for time cards and clerical labor. Also, the accounts do not always correctly reflect the true measure of the effort. Financial control is no substitute for close communication in information research and it is often counterproductive in achieving the greatest utilization of human, and other resources.

We now come to the first of the examples which may illustrate, in the homiest way possible, what I am trying to convey.

A company is seeking a permit to operate a storage facility for desulfurized heavy fuel oil. The questions are: first, what are the present emissions into the atmosphere, and secondly what measures are required to bring these emissions to within the statutory requirements. We have available to us the drawing of storage vessels, the plat, and the properties normally specified for heavy fuel oil, density, viscosity, flash point, and heating value. We also know the storage temperature of the fuel.

The emissions are primarily hydrocarbons and they occur because of the partial pressure of the components of the fuel in the air space between the liquid surface and the roof. When a storage tank is refilled the air in this space is displaced and leaves through vents in the roof. Air is expelled also from the "breathing" which occurs because of the daily variation of the ambient air temperature.

There are accepted formulas for calculating the emissions from both of these sources and they have been long used for estimating losses in gasoline storage. The formulas require a knowledge, however, of the vapor pressure of the fuel at the storage temperature. Vapor pressure is commonly specified for gasoline (as the Reid vapor pressure) but it is "not available" for heavy fuel oil.

Now the consequences of "not available" is that you cannot properly characterize the proposed emission and therefore you probably cannot prosecute the application for the permit. Therefore, "not available" is also "not acceptable." Happily, the vapor pressures of hydrocarbons are related to their flash points. I will not enter into any details except to point out that for many of the hydrocarbons which would be expected to occur in the air over a heavy fuel oil, the minimum concentration in air to propagate an explosion is about 1% by volume of the hydrocarbon.

We may assume therefore, that the commonly used Pensky-Martin flash point is the temperature at which the vapor pressure is equal to approximately 1% of one atmosphere (7.6 mm). Now there are some very reliable formulas for extrapolation of the vapor pressure at the temperature of storage (125°F.) from the 7.6 mm at the temperature which is specified at the flash point. This permits estimation of the rate of emission per hour, in mols. Finally, to put this problem to bed we must make a reasonable assumption of the mean molecular weight of the hydrocarbons in the vapor to come up with the emissions estimated in pounds as required in the emissions statement which must accompany the application for the permit.

If any here wish to question an estimate made in this way, I can only say that if I have, in my professional judgement, made an estimate which is conservatively stated and if the emissions, thus estimated, are not a major contributing factor in ambient air quality, then I am justified.

It is often essential, in the environmental study of water resources, to have access to many physical and chemical properties which are "not available." I could mention, just in passing, solubilities, absorption isotherms, surface activity, reaction rates, thermodynamic properties, diffusivities, etc., etc. All of these and more: just find the ones you need.

Environmental.information science is much more than access to tables of data and catalogues of formulas. It is more properly an art of utilizing all the resources which are justified: all of the retrieval systems and anything else that can contribute to obtaining the most accurate and reliable information which is possible within the total constraints.

The quest for information in environmental science encompasses not only physical and chemical properties and system performance but also information regarding environmental impact and economic impact. Both of these may again be illustrated by homey examples which are selected at random as fairly typical, though admittedly, probably remote from the area of interest to all of you.

Addition of a heavy metal salt to a municipal drinking water supply is not likely to be accepted without convincing evidence that this is not inimical to human health. Suppose then that your assignment is to assemble all of the information relating to the effect of this heavy metal on human health.

The normal response to this assignment is to retrieve all of the publications dealing with the toxicology of the metal and then cite the opinions of the authors. This is a case in which the normal is not necessarily the most logical approach, nor one which is best designed to influence environmental authorities in the direction of favorable action. What is the alternative?

In the first place we should seek the information regarding all of the physiological and chemical transformations of the metal from ingestion to excretion and, if it is retained, the organs or tissue, and the chemical form, of its retention.

One should next determine whether the metal is a normal constituent of foodstuffs and, if it is, the concentrations and the average and probable maximum amount normally ingested.

One should determine, if possible, the functional role, if any, of the metal in metabolic or immunological processes of the body or in the synthesis of the enzyme systems which regulate these processes. This role may be positive, i.e., one in which the metal is physiologically essential or it may be negative, i.e., one in which the metal impedes the metabolic or immunologic processes. Finally, we may require a knowledge of the symptoms and consequences, if any, of chronic and acute toxicity as well as of the symptoms and consequences, if any, of a dietary deficiency of the metal both in man and animals.

This listing is not presented as an exhaustive characterization of the requirement for information relative to the appraisal of environmental effect. It is, however, a reasonable basis for such an appraisal and perhaps illustrates the extent to which the environmental information specialist should be prepared to go.

As a final example of the search for environmental information I have selected one from the field of economics. Suppose that the task assigned is to project for a given market area the quantity of desulfurized heavy fuel oil which can be sold at various levels of price.

We need to know, first, the emission standards for sulfur oxides from power, and space heating boiler furnaces of various categories, according to the recognized state, county or municipal codes. Next we need to know the projected consumption of fuel in the various power networks and heating facilities. We need to take into consideration the effect of all local laws governing the sulfur content of fuel. State and federal legislation, both enacted and pending, must be taken into account. Finally, we must evaluate the potential of processes under development for removal of sulfur oxides from flue gas. An economic evaluation of such processes is necessary to estimate the maximum price for desulfurized fuel. This is the price above which it is more economical to use fuel of usual sulfur content in combination with a system for removal of the oxides of sulfur from the combustion products.

There are several publications which summarize current legislation in environmental matters as well as current enforcement actions and decisions of the courts and commissions. For information regarding fuel consumption it is necessary to refer to the state Public Service Commissions which hold information in their files. It is public information which is available to anyone who will call at the offices of a commission. Although the information is public it is not published and therefore it is not distributed on request. It is possible, however, to obtain copies of special economic reports prepared for the guidance of the commission in its primary function of setting schedules of rates for power and fuel sold by public utilities. Some of these reports analyze and project the impact on utility costs of various imminent or anticipated changes of operation in conformance with environmental requirements.

It is worth our while to dwell on the matter of economic impact of environmentally related developments because these are becoming so extremely important to every segment of industry. They affect the costs of materials, the costs of manufacture, the costs of utilities; they affect the competitive position within an industry and between competing industries, they affect the markets for commodities, equipment and systems.

It is a certainty that there will be a tremendous need for information sources to guide both industry and government in projections for the purpose of policy determination and planning. This will require the fullest employment of all libraries and other sources of information as well as the best exercise of judgement by professional information researchers.

This judgement is required in the evaluation of information as well as in its retrieval or synthesis. In the vast expansion of published information there is, unfortunately a corresponding expansion of exaggerated claims in press releases, distortions, propaganda and sheer irresponsibility. Most of what is published is valueless, or worse. This is true of respected journals which manifest increasingly a tendency to regard circulation and advertising volume as their concerns to the virtual exclusion of a scrupulous regard for a conservative presentation of forecast and opinion and an exact representation of what purports to be fact. Most journals are now edited with the thought that they will be read once and then discarded. This is not usually conducive to a concern that statements may be reread critically against a background of advance knowledge and experience.

It is necessary, as a consequence, to evaluate the reliability of information given unless there is substantiating data or reference to primary sources which may be verified. Statistical information, including that of project costs, is usually accurate but cost projections are often grossly inaccurate, usually in the direction of understatement. There is also a tendency on the part of authors who represent vendors to understate operating problems such as fouling, corrosion and undue maintenance costs. Especially unreliable is published information derived from the press releases of promoters of new processes or from enterprises in which technical details are sparse or lacking.

From the papers of this symposium you will be given closer looks at the many sources of environmental information from the several viewpoints of librarian, editor, specialist in governmental sources and industry association. One may reasonably assume that from a consideration of these diverse viewpoints one may obtain a broad perspective of the problem of environmental information. One may assume also that there may be some seeming inconsistencies and even contradictions in these views. This afternoon, after the delivery of all the papers, their contents will be explored by a panel which will question the speakers to resolve, if possible, some of these differences or, at least, to delineate them more clearly. At the conclusion of this panel discussion there will be questions from the audience.

RESOURCES AND INDUSTRIAL COOPERATION
ON ENVIRONMENTAL CONTROL
AT THE AMERICAN PETROLEUM INSTITUTE

E.H. Brenner
Manager, Central Abstracting and Indexing Service
American Petroleum Institute
New York, New York

The petroleum industry's concern for the environment is not new.
The API's organized efforts to deal with pollution problems go back
some 45 years - - to 1927 when the Committee on Refinery
Environmental Control (originally called the Committee on Disposal
of Refinery Wastes) was established. As its name implies, this group
has been concerned with pollution control problems and practices at
refineries. Its most important single achievement has been the development and continuing revision of the Manual on Disposal of
Refinery Wastes. The manual represents the current state of control
technology and deals with air, water, and solid wastes.

At the end of World War II, a second committee was formed with
the API Division of Refining to handle other air and water pollution
problems. This committee concerned itself with control of pollution resulting from petroleum industry operations and from the use
of petroleum products. It sponsored a program of research that
from the mid-fifties to the mid-sixties cost more than $2 million.

A third API committee, the Central Committee on Medicine and
Health, long concerned itself with aspects of the air pollution problem within its field of interest.

In 1964, still another committee was created to provide a connect-
ing link between the three committees named above and other API
components, including the Committee on Public Affairs, which were
also involved in activities related to air and water conservation. Its
members included representatives from all appropriate segments of

9

the Institute plus liaison members from other oil industry associations.

Early in 1965, recognizing society's steadily growing concern for the quality of our environment, the API Board of Directors named a special ad hoc committee to study all of the Institute's conservation efforts and to make recommendations for streamlining and accelerating those efforts.

This committee recommended both a series of projects for consideration and the creation of a permanent committee that would have major status within the API. The Committee's recommendations were approved by the Board in November 1965 and the Committee for Air and Water Conservation (CAWC) was born. For its first year, CAWC was budgeted at almost $2 million for conservation research expenditures. Each year since 1969, CAWC has been budgeted at over $3 million.

CAWC consists of representatives from 20 API member companies: men chosen for their experience in research, refining, marketing, transportation, production, medicine, and public affairs. Other major oil industry associations also send liaison representatives to CAWC meetings.

Working under CAWC are two committees directly responsible for carrying out the research program. These are the Engineering and Technical Research Committee (E&TRC) and the Health and Biological Research Committee (H&BRC). E&TRC is made up of industry representatives who have important air and water conservation responsibilities within their respective companies. H&BRC consists primarily of oil company physicians who have expertise in biology and related fields.

The Coordinating Research Council (CRC) represents the outgrowth of almost 50 years of mutual endeavor between the automotive and petroleum industries to improve vehicle equipment, fuels, and lubricants. CRC efforts have contributed to significant advances in technology designed to reduce atmospheric pollution caused by vehicle emissions.

In the Fall of 1967, the Air Pollution Research Advisory Committee (APRAC) was formed within the Coordinating Research Council to launch a major program of research on automotive air pollution. APRAC is composed of technical and medical experts from the petroleum and automotive industries and from the U.S. Environmental Protection Agency (EPA).

Funding for APRAC is shared equally between the Automobile Manufacturers Association and the American Petroleum Institute. On a selective basis, EPA contributes financial support to a majority of the projects and shares in the direction of all projects. The research is carried out under contracts with various universities, medical schools, government laboratories, and private research organizations.

The purpose of the APRAC program is not to develop automotive hardware or special petroleum products, but rather to provide basic information on the nature and effects of vehicle air pollution. The program covers subjects of mutual interest to industry and to the government and is divided into three main areas of research:

> engineering projects which explore the interactions between petroleum products and the automotive equipment in which the products are used (CAPE Projects);

> atmospheric projects aimed at explaining pollutant behavior in the atmosphere (CAPA Projects);

> medical projects to determine the effect of automotive emissions upon health (CAPM Projects).

The data acquired from these investigations are expected to provide industry with the technical information needed to achieve further reduction of emissions through the development of improved equipment and petroleum products. The data are also expected to assist the government in establishing air quality standards and emission control requirements.

API's Wildlife Conservation Liaison Committee came into being in 1960 with a mandate to establish and maintain liaison with national conservation leaders in an effort to resolve major environmental problems of mutual concern. The issues and activities that have been freely and frankly discussed in the past have included: leasing and drilling for oil and gas on public lands, particularly in wilderness and wildlife areas; air and water pollution and land conservation; billboards on highway systems and highway beautification; marine drilling operations; the use of pesticides and insecticides; operation of the Bureau of Mines; the Alaska pipeline; the Big Cypress Swamp in Florida; and the need for a long-range national energy and fuels policy.

In addition to its liaison work with conservation organizations, the Committee also works with the Department of the Interior and other agencies and organizations on conservation matters. Annually, it has a top-level meeting with the Secretary of Interior and his staff and other conservation leaders. Through these meetings, the Committee seeks constantly to keep government and conservation organizations informed about what the industry is doing in the field of environmental management and pollution control.

The Committee also sponsors two national scholarship programs, one with the National Wildlife Federation, the other with the Wildlife Management Institute. Although the programs were just initiated, two PhD. projects are now in progress. Matching grants are made to the organizations from a fund approved by API in 1970.

A special information source activity in which API is involved is related to the storage and retrieval of information in the air and water conservation area and goes on in the Central Abstracting and Indexing Service of the American Petroleum Institute. This operation began 18 years ago as a centralized abstracting service designed to cover information that the petroleum industry would originally be doing for themselves and thereby saving them considerable money. Today the abstracting and indexing services produced is a $1 million operation totally paid for by subscriptions mainly from petroleum companies. The main abstracting publication today is called Abstracts of Refining Literature.

A full professional force of chemists and chemical engineers read technical articles in more than 150 English-language, Russian, German, Italian, French, and Polish periodicals. In the course of a year they find about 20,000 items reporting new scientific and technical developments, engineering work, and other material of importance to the petroleum refining and petrochemical industry. API Abstracts of Refining Literature promptly brings these items to the attention of its readers.

The bulletins of abstracts are distributed to the subscriber weekly. Each abstract is delivered within three to four weeks after receipt of the source document. The informative abstract contains from one to two hundred words; each abstract transmitting the main information contained in the item reported, so that the subscriber can easily decide whether he needs to read the original. But even when he chooses not to look at the source document, the reader is informed of the main news. Grouping the abstracts by subject within each issue of the bulletin allows the reader to find quickly the material that specifically interests him by looking at only a fraction of the abstracts printed. There are four major subject groups to API Abstracts of Refining Literature. One of these major groupings is the Bulletin on Air and Water Conservation. This separate abstract publication on air and water conservation is broken down under the following subject headings:

Air pollution sources	Physical/chemical properties
Water pollution sources	of water
Atmospheric interaction	Economic factor
Air pollution control	Air quality measurement
Water pollution control	Water quality measurement
Measurement methods	Legal considerations
Health	Standardization
Plants	Science/technology
Animals	Public relations
Materials	

As far as cost of the publication on air and water conservation is concerned, petroleum companies are expected to subscribe to the total publication, API Abstracts of Refining Literature, and thus the subscription for the total package runs from $13,000 to $2,500 depending on the gross assets of the subscribing petroleum company.

Non-petroleum companies need not subscribe to the four bulletins and if a non-petroleum company is interested in the air and water conservation abstract publication, the subscriber pays $550 per year if the company has gross assets in excess of $0.1 billion, $275 per year if less than $0.1 million, and $275 per year if a non-profit organization. This publication is weekly and contains approximately 75 abstracts per week. These abstracts are indexed, but are not available unless the total index of the Refining Literature is subscribed to. This then makes it rather expensive for a non-petroleum company who must pay from $3,000 to $6,000 depending on its size for subscriptions.

Recently, however, the Central Abstracting and Indexing Service has made an agreement with Petroleum Publishing Company to advertize and sell searches of its file and any search of all information abstracted and indexed at API since 1964, is now available. A search of this eight-year file costs $150 and contains approximately 150,000 abstracts of which about 12,000 are related to air and water conservation.

In addition, an SDI service is available which would allow you to profile your specific interests related to air and water conservation and, on a monthly basis, a list of references related to your interests would be delivered to you based on the abstracts that API would have done for a specific month. Twelve listings for the year would cost $125.00.

The petroleum industry's concern for the environment will continue and research recorded in words will continue to be documented and indexed through API's CAWC (The Committee on Air and Water Conservation) and CAIS (Central Abstracting and Indexing Service).

This paper includes excerpts from "Environmental Research — A Status Report," a staff paper by the Committee for Air and Water Conservation and the Committee on Public Affairs of the American Petroleum Institute. January 1972.

ENVIRONMENTAL PROTECTION AGENCY
AND ITS R&D PROGRAM

William J. Lacy
Chief, Applied Science and Technology
Office of Research and Monitoring
Environmental Protection Agency
Washington, D.C.

Never in the history of this country has any movement caught on so fast as the wave of environmentalism that has swept over our people during these last two or three years.

The average citizen — that includes anyone who has ever breathed foul air, observed the turbid flow of our filthy rivers, or driven a car in traffic; anyone who has ever tried to find a little peace and quiet; anyone who has ever had doubts about the purity of his food and drink — this average citizen demands action on the part of business and government to clean up the mess we have made.

Our problems with pollution are not new. Indeed, man has abused the environment as long as mankind has been on this planet, but in recent years population growth has exceeded the capacity of our air and water to absorb the municipal and industrial pollutants, and we can no longer turn our backs on the problems we have created.

In the past we did not fully appreciate what we were doing to our air and water resources. We ignored the fact that these are finite and limited resources, although our demands upon them have increased at alarming rates. Consider that, since 1900, the population of the United States has doubled and that in this same period of time the needs of industry for water have increased ten times. It is estimated that the next doubling of the world population will occur in 35 years rather than 70 and we can anticipate similar industrial growth.

It is clear that we must take immediate action to restore the environment to the quality we expect and demand. We have made progress. New technology has been developed for treatment of air pollutants and liquid wastes but sometimes the treatment of one has been to the detriment of the other. Further, our population and industrial growth have outstripped our technology in many cases and, despite the installation of required treatment facilities, we have found a decline in stream quality in many parts of the United States.

BACKGROUND OF THE FEDERAL WATER POLLUTION CONTROL PROGRAM

In the last few years, there have been several important changes in the Federal water pollution control program. As a matter of fact, I know of no other Federal program that has been subjected to more changes in such a short period of time. The milestone Water Quality Act of 1965 provided for state water quality standards for the first time in Federal legislation and established the Federal Water Pollution Control Administration.

This was followed by transfer of the new agency to the Department of the Interior, and the enactment of the Clean Water Restoration Act in 1966. The latter provided not only a vastly increased authorization for Federal grants for construction of sewage plants, but also for research and demonstration of new or improved ideas in the municipal and industrial joint waste treatment field. On December 2, 1970, the President reorganized this entire office into one central agency dealing with environmental pollution problems; the new agency is the Environmental Protection Agency.

Let me speak for a moment on the reasons for the reorganization to form EPA. In the past the organization of the Federal Government to deal with pollution has suffered from two obvious problems. First, for many particular kinds of pollution, a number of different Federal agencies have had overlapping or closely related responsibilities. For example, three Federal Departments (Agriculture, HEW, and Interior) were directly involved in regulating pesticides. Similarly, a number of agencies have responsibilities for radiation problems.

Secondly, the organizational basis for controlling pollution was neither consistent nor adequate. The two largest agencies, the Federal Water

Quality Administration and the National Air Pollution Control Administration, were organized on the basis of the media, air or water, through which the pollutants traveled. The remaining pollution control programs on the other hand, generally were organized on the basis of pollutants, pesticides, radioactive materials, and solid wastes.

Research on ecological effects must consider the interrelated parts of the environment and the impact of man's activities on them. It will be far easier to conduct ecological studies in an agency which is not limited to one particular medium or pollutant. Likewise, waste treatment research may now consider integrated systems to control air and water pollution and the ultimate disposal or recycling of solid wastes.

Hopefully, this discussion of the Federal water pollution control programs, especially the R&D program, may indicate areas of mutual participation and cooperation by and between the Federal, state, municipal, and industrial authorities.

THE EPA

The Environmental Protection Agency is one of the youngest branches of the Federal Government, only 16 months old, but already it is one of the best known and most widely publicized. Hardly a day goes by when the newspapers and television and radio news programs contain no mention of EPA's enforcement actions; 180-day notices; standard-setting activities, and so on.

This high visibility, of course, is a tribute not only to the energy and dedication of Bill Ruckelshaus, the Administrator, and his EPA team, but it also reflects the strong public concern over environmental problems. The agency is guided and pushed by a great grass roots movement to do something about the environmental mess we are in. Never before have the American people been so united over a peacetime issue as they are now united in the cause of a better environment.

The Agency is charged by the Congress and by Executive Order of the President with leading the Federal Government's efforts to protect environmental values, to halt pollution wherever possible, and to perform and sponsor research to promote these ends.

It is important to realize that the EPA is primarily a regulating and enforcement Agency. Congress has adopted specific laws regarding air pollution, water pollution, solid waste disposal, pesticides, and radiation protection that EPA is obliged to carry out. These laws antedate the formation of EPA. The programs of standards-setting, grants administration, etc. were well under way when the President decided to unify the Federal efforts toward environmental control into one independent agency divorced from any concern with promoting any particular sector of the economy.

That independence is very important. The old-line agencies tend to become identified with the activities they must regulate, for example, the Agriculture Department promotes farm production and efficiency and the AEC promotes the use of nuclear power. To have them set standards for pesticides and radiation in the environment raises questions of conflict of interest and credibility.

As a Federal Agency, EPA is not big and doesn't have a lot of money. They employ about 8,300 people and their current budget is about $2.5 billion. $2 billion of this, i.e., about four-fifths, is earmarked for sewage treatment facilities in the form of aid to localities for their design and construction. The actual operating budget this year is about $450 million. Slightly more than one-fourth of that is for research and monitoring.

EPA is not a new Department of Defense research and engineering agency, not a new NASA, and not a new science foundation. As I said, the EPA is a regulatory and enforcement agency, and in EPA, research and technology are for the purpose of making possible realistic and effective regulatory, control and enforcement programs for environmental pollution. Because our state of knowledge on pollution effects and abatement technology is so very limited and in such an elementary state, the research program of EPA is necessarily a large and very active component of the Agency mission.

Within EPA the Office of Research and Monitoring has two primary objectives: to provide a sound base of scientific knowledge for regulatory environmental standards and enforcement actions; and to develop and demonstrate effective and economically practical ways to aid pollution-damaged environments and methods for recovery and use of discharged resources and by-products of pollution treatment.

The basic philosophy in carrying out this research and technological advancement work is the anticipation that the results will be used for problem solving. About 70% of the work is engineering oriented, that is, it mainly employs empirical methodology and existing scientific knowledge. About 20% might be regarded as basic research in that it is directed toward the acquisition of new knowledge and scientific understanding, and about 10% is for the analysis of the effects of our technological society on the environment and the identification of pollution control methods.

Six months ago the research and technological programs were a collection of pieces and parts from the 15 inherited organizations. Today EPA is in the final phases of centralizing its organization. Most of the research and demonstration problems are now under the direct control of the ORM. This assures the programs' relevance to the Agency's mission functions, and assures that long-term research goals are worked on so that when problems do arise, they do not come as a surprise.

In the last six months the research programs of all the predecessor organizations have been separated and differentiated. They have been integrated into a new pattern of functions that are output oriented, and the first mode of new research program management relationships and procedures has been developed. The 40 or so inherited laboratories and 100-odd field sites have been restructured into a four-unit national system which emphasizes interdisciplinary skills and facilities applied to comprehensive and systematic treatment of total environmental problems.

The Office of Research and Monitoring presently consists of about 1,500 people. About 70% of our staff are professional scientists and engineers and nearly 20% are people at the doctoral level. Of the budgeted $120 million per year, about $38 million goes for in-house work, i.e., it pays for the salaries of our people, laboratory facilities, test equipment, purchase of operating supplies and services. About $45 million goes for contract work to supplement our in-house activities, and another $35 million goes for research grants. About $2 million goes for transfers to other Government agencies to help us do our job.

The organization is simple and straightforward. There are two offices to determine and supervise technical programs, namely, Office of Research and the Office of Monitoring, and one office to provide the wherewithal to carry out the program, namely, the Office of Program Operations. The real action in our program is at our four field units, three of which have been designated as National

Environmental Research Centers, the fourth as an independent laboratory. There is a National Center in Cincinnati with a system of satellite laboratories whose principal mission is pollution abatement technology and engineering. We have another National Center at Corvallis, Oregon, again with satellite laboratories, where the principal thrust is ecological analysis and the environmental effects of pollution. Still another National Center is at Research Triangle Park, North Carolina, whose main concern is environmental health effects. The fourth or independent laboratory, the Western Environmental Research Laboratory at Las Vegas, has as its mission radiation effects, monitoring and control.

I'd like to describe the nature of our research program in a broad way. First, we are concerned about acquiring knowledge on the sources, movement and fate of pollutants, to provide insight into where control actions can be most effectively applied. We are studying these movements in air, water, land, and living organisms, the interchanges between these systems, the changes in pollutants, and interactions among pollutants.

Next, we are studying the effects of pollutants on man and on the resources he needs or wants to provide knowledge of what amounts of pollutants, acting singly or together, produce what kinds of effects. The pollutants being studied include industrial wastes and trash, chemicals, noise, and radiation (both ionizing and nonionizing). The effects being studied include health; atmospheric changes as they affect climate and weather; and changes in individual or populations of living organisms. Disciplines include epidemiology; toxicology both human and animal; ecology; and economics and other social sciences.

Work in monitoring includes development of both sampling techniques and devices for use in research and in surveillance. We are engaged in determination of base line conditions as a basis for gauging changes in amounts of pollutants, condition of the environment, and functioning of ecological systems.

A major thrust of our work is concerned with the development of prevention and/or control techniques and systems for dealing with pollution in and from municipalities, agricultural activities, manufacturing, power generation, transportation, mining, recreational activities, and accidental spills of oil and hazardous materials. Our work is conducted both in-house, cooperatively with the private sector or with other Government agencies, and through contracts and grants to make use of whatever capabilities are best suited to the problems.

Grant Program — Industrial Participation

Industry may participate in these grant programs for the construction of permanent waste treatment facilities on industry property to foster the development of and to demonstrate new or improved methods of treating industrial wastes or otherwise prevent pollution, in the hope that these methods shall have industrywide application. Grants so authorized may not exceed 70% of the project cost, up to $1 million.

The Federal Water Pollution Control Act, as amended, also provides grants for projects which can develop and demonstrate "new or improved methods of joint treatment systems for municipal and industrial wastes". Capital advantages are certainly possible if industries can discharge their wastes into municipal systems.

The grants program represents a truly cooperative effort; it is a cost-sharing type of contract. However, in some of EPA's research and development, the Federal Government bears the full cost, contracting with appropriate nongovernment entities for these services. Limited funds are available for this purpose. Through the contract device, EPA can support almost any related worthwhile project under almost any type of institutional arrangement. We have the means for assisting pilot-scale demonstration and large, full-scale projects.

To receive a grant two basic conditions must be met: the project must have scientific and technical merit and there must be technical competence associated with the project whether provided by the grantee himself or by consultants who he employs; and the project activities must usefully demonstrate a way to combat water pollution. The results of these projects must be accurate in terms of both cost and performance and they must be made available to the public.

WATERBORNE WASTES OF INDUSTRIAL ORIGIN

The estimated volume of wastewater discharged by industry (excluding power generating stations) is approximately 36 billion gallons per day. Four basic industries account for 80 to 85% of this total. The breakdown of wastewater discharges is as follows.

	Billion gal./day	Percent
Basic metals (mostly steel)	7.7	21.5
Chemicals	7.8	22
Pulp and paper	6.6	18.5
Petroleum	7.2	20
Food	1.4	4
Textiles	1.2	3.2
Others	4.1	10.8
Total	36.0	100.0

Conventional treatment technology is often inadequate for many types of industrial wastes. Techniques must be developed which must be shown to achieve effective and economical control of wastes from these six major water-using manufacturing areas which account for more than 80% of all water used by industry. The extent of their future needs can be estimated from growth forecasts for the next decade: iron and steel, 37%; chemicals, 140%; pulp and paper, 68%; nonferrous metals, 55%; petroleum, 53%; and food, 35%.

The National Association of Manufacturers estimates that to achieve control of industry's water pollution, another $8 billion, or nearly eight times the value of existing control facilities, will have to be spent by 1978. If new technology is not developed, then much of this investment will be in outmoded plants which are not capable of meeting ever-more-stringent effluent. requirements.

So the question may be raised at this point whether our economy, oriented toward production and consumption per se, can accommodate new social requirements and do so at a reasonable cost.

At first glance, pollution control looks like a prohibitively expensive proposition. For example, in our annual EPA report to Congress on the economics of clean air we forecast expenditures of around $42 billion in the period fiscal 1973-77 just to control air pollution alone. The Council on Environmental Quality estimated that the combined cost to industry and government of air and water cleanup plus better management of solid wastes would amount to around $105 billion between 1970-75, in other words, about 1% of the cumulative gross national product in those years.

But this Administration recognized at the outset that we needed additional independent confirmation of the total dollar cost of a national effort to clean up the air and the water. Last year the Council on Environmental Quality, the Department of Commerce and the Environmental Protection Agency commissioned a task force of impartial consultants to get the answers.

The results of their computer study were released on March 13, and I think they should be reassuring to all who have wondered whether this nation can actually afford the costs of a major environmental renovation. The panel analyzed eleven major industry groups and found that current pollution control requirements would compel the closing of 200 to 300 plants by the end of 1976. However, none of the eleven will be hurt severely as a whole.

Most of the 12,000 plants now operating will stay in business and be profitable, 800 are expected to close down due to obsolescence or other reasons not connected with environment. Our task force estimates that the overwhelming majority of plants that will close to avoid installation of expensive pollution control equipment would fold up anyway in the period 1976-80 because they are outmoded and unprofitable.

The ultimate goal of the EPA, in cooperation with industry whenever possible, is to develop and demonstrate alternative economical treatment techniques and advanced waste treatment systems directed toward closed-loop systems.

EPA intends to develop and demonstrate the necessary treatment techniques for significant industrial wastewaters to the extent necessary to meet water quality criteria and eventually to permit total water reuse. According to the Census Bureau, there are more than 315,000 manufacturing establishments in the country. A little over 3% of these, or only 9,000 to 10,000, account for 97% of all the water used by U.S. industry.

For the purposes of our discussion let us define wastes as the momentarily unusable product of human industry. I say momentarily because all wastes have use in some time frame and in some ecosystem. The time frame is impacted by technology and need. I point out "unusable" because man does not willingly throw away his assets.

Time, need, place, and technology then, all determine the scope of the industrial waste problem. Yesterday's moldy bread is today's penicillin. Last month's paper mill wastes could be in tomorrow's road binding materials, cooking sauces, or medicinals. An oil refinery in the water-rich eastern states, using and then discharging copious amounts of cooling water, produces no better grade of product than the refinery in the arid West which was compelled to be designed to utilize one-half to one-third the amount of water in its head exchange systems. Some industrial plants have proceeded to close their waste-water systems.

The goal of any research program is to provide through technical investigation the criteria upon which decisions can be based to solve the problem. In the case of industrial waste treatment research, these criteria may be design criteria for waste treatment facilities. Note that I did not indicate that the research need is to set treatment standards since this may involve social and economic considerations as well as technological requirements developed by us as researchers.

Dr. Greenfield, the Assistant Administrator for R&M recently stated that it is our job to provide the best possible technical input upon which sound decisions can be based in the standard setting process. President Nixon, in his message to Congress last year on a program for a better environment, said, "We have the technology now to deal with most forms of water pollution. We must make sure that it is used." This does not mean that our job is done, only that a solution is available. Obviously, Henry Ford's Model T provided a solution to the transportation problem. Fortunately development of the automobile did not stop there.

GOVERNMENT SOURCES OF INFORMATION
ON ENVIRONMENTAL CONTROL

Marshall Sittig
Director of Special Projects
Princeton University
Princeton, New Jersey

The environment has become an important concern of the Federal Government; hence, the Federal apparatus has become a major source of information on environmental control.

The Federal involvement with the environment dates back many years. Indeed, the Refuse Act of 1899, promulgated by the Corps of Engineers of the United States Army for preserving the navigability of waterways, has been on the books for many years and recently furnished the basis for Department of Justice complaints against chlor-alkali manufacturers for mercury pollution.

Recent Federal involvement with the environment has centered on the creation of two bodies.

(1) The policy-making Council on Environmental Quality which was established by the National Environmental Policy Act of 1969, "to formulate and recommend national policies to promote the improvement of the environment." This Council is chaired by Russel E. Train and is located across from the White House at 722 Jackson Place, N.W., Washington, D.C. 20006. The Council issues an annual report which is full of good summary data and is well referenced with bibliographies.

(2) The policy-implementing operating agency, the Environmental Protection Agency (or EPA as it is

known). EPA was established in the Executive Branch as an independent agency pursuant to Reorganization Plan 3 of 1970, effective December 2, 1970. It includes the air-pollution control and solid wastes disposal as well as the radiological health and water hygiene programs which had been in the Dept. of Health, Education and Welfare (HEW) and the water pollution control program which had been in the Department of the Interior.

U.S. PATENT OFFICE

As regards sources of information on environmental control, the first of these to be considered here is that of United States Patents. This author has long held that such patents are among the prime source of timely technological information.

The availability of patents and information on patents is reasonably common knowledge but will be reviewed briefly here. Each Tuesday, the Official Gazette of the United States Patent Office is issued. It costs $89 per year on a subscription basis and gives abstracts of some 1,700 patents every week divided into mechanical, chemical and electrical categories.

From reading the abstract or by searching individual patent classes at the Patent Office in Crystal Plaza in Alexandria, Virginia (Class 55 for Gas Separation or Class 210 for Liquid Purification or Separation for example) one can ascertain one's interest in a particular patent.

Copies can then be ordered by number alone from the United States Patent Office for 50¢ each, regardless of length. Mail orders take several weeks to fill and copies are more expeditiously obtained by using coupons purchased at the office in Building 3 of Crystal Plaza in Alexandria, Virginia out near Washington National Airport. Service on these coupons is available to box-holders at the office on a 24-48 hour basis. Temporary boxes may be had at no charge for short term use for the asking. Patent lawyers and professional patent searchers have permanent boxes which they rent for $12 per year.

The importance of United States Patents in the pollution abatement area has been highlighted by an order from President Nixon early in 1970 to expedite applications for patents on all inventions that will "materially enhance" the quality of the environment. It is estimated that this special treatment will cut the waiting time between application and issue of such patents from three years to about six months.

The then Commissioner of Patents, William Schuyler, estimated that 5% of the 300,000 patents awaiting action in early 1970 would be subject to the expediting order on the basis of their relevance to the environment. The special designation is not automatic; the applicant must explain how his invention will contribute to the environmental cause.

In early 1972, the present Commissioner, Robert Gottschalk, was asked to consider whether other priority "new technology" areas such as energy sources, mass transit and drug abuse would also receive priority treatment in the Patent Office. He indicated that they would not. However, across the board speedup is being attempted with pollution control remaining the only priority area.

GOVERNMENT PRINTING OFFICE

The second general source of information on environmental control to be discussed here is publications from the Superintendent of Documents, the United States Government Printing Office. Here information on publications is perhaps best available from the biweekly "Selected Government Publications" which is available by mail at no charge upon request.

The prices of GPO publications vary widely from a few cents to a few dollars but they usually are very low in cost considering the content.

The sources of GPO manuscript material may be EPA, the Congress or any of various Government departments or departmental subdivisions such as the National Industrial Pollution Control Council which will be discussed later in this paper.

NATIONAL TECHNICAL INFORMATION SERVICE

The third general source of environmental information to be discussed here is that organ of the Department of Commerce now known as the National Technical Information Service. This is the organization which used to be known as the Clearinghouse for Federal Scientific and Technical Information.

It started out life as the agency which disseminated the reports from captured German industrial intelligence after World War II, the Office of Technical Services. It then became the conduit for a wide variety of Government reports and now constitutes one of the most important sources of environmental information.

For entree to NTIS reports on the environment, there are various avenues open.

(1)   For $5.00 per year one could until recently subscribe to a semimonthly <u>Environmental Reports Topical Announcements</u> bulletin in the category of environmental pollution and control. This abstracts many environmental impact statements, delineating the effect of highway construction in a specific area on the local flora and fauna, an area of little interest to chemists and engineers in general. It also abstracts other Government publications available through NTIS (usually so-called PB reports in the categories of:

(a)   air pollution and control
(b)   noise pollution and control
(c)   solid waste pollution and control
(d)   water pollution and control.

It lists prices for microfiche copies when available and for soft copies from NTIS (or sometimes from the GPO).

Starting in April 1972, a new <u>Weekly Government Abstract</u> series has become available at $22.50 per year, replacing the semimonthly publication in the area of environmental pollution and control.

(2)   There has been one collective bibliography published (May 1970) bearing the title of "Environmental Pollution -- A Selective Bibliography," Report PB-192318 at $3.00 per copy. Unfortunately, this publication has not been updated.

(3)   Custom subject searches are available from NTIS at the cost of $25 per 100 abstracts or fraction thereof.

(4)   Search "packages" are available from NTIS on such

topics as odor pollution, noise pollution, and hazardous waste disposal.

Publications from NTIS are available at a set of standardized prices in multiples of $3. The cost is $3 for 0 to 300 pages, $6 for a copy of a publication of 301 to 600 pages and $9 for a copy of a publication of over 601 pages.

Publications from NTIS may be ordered by calling (703)-321-8543. If one has a deposit account they will be mailed at no additional cost. Otherwise they may be ordered on a ship and bill basis. They may also be picked up at NTIS in Springfield, Virginia or at Room 1098 of the Department of Commerce building, E Street entrance at 14th Street, N.W., Washington, D.C.

ENVIRONMENTAL PROTECTION AGENCY (EPA)

The fourth category of environmental information to be considered is reports published by EPA.

Since EPA is in the process of consolidating a variety of report-issuing points of various qualities, rates of productivity and geographical locations, the picture is a confused and confusing one.

Thus, a comprehensive report on mercury pollution was published in November 1970 as a joint publication of EPA and HEW. I learned of its existence from a brief note in one of the weeklies, Chemical and Engineering News or Chemical Week, and upon going to the public information office of EPA then located at 1626 K Street in Washington, I obtained a copy free of charge. Finding it was a strict bibliographic accident, however.

As EPA becomes more consolidated in its new agency headquarters location at Waterside Mall, 4th and M Streets, S.W., Washington, D.C. 20460 it will hopefully present a more uniform and comprehensible face to the information-seeking public.

It now has a Research Information Division in the office of Research and Monitoring at that headquarters location. That office will coordinate the following offices dealing with various technical areas.

(1) Publications Branch (water)
     Research Information Division
     Environmental Protection Agency
     Washington, D.C. 20460

(2) Air Pollution Technical Information Center
     Office of Technical Information and Publications
     Office of Air Programs
     Environmental Protection Agency
     Research Triangle Park, North Carolina 27711

(3) Publications Distribution Unit
     Office of Solid Waste Management Programs
     Environmental Protection Agency
     555 Ridge Avenue
     Cincinnati, Ohio 45213

(4) Information Section
     Division of Pesticides Community Studies
     Office of Pesticides Programs
     Environmental Protection Agency
     4770 Buford Highway
     Chamblee, Georgia 30341

(5) Technical Publications Officer - Radiation Publications
     Twinbrook Research Laboratory
     Environmental Protection Agency
     Rockville, Maryland 20460

OFFICE OF SCIENCE AND TECHNOLOGY

The fifth category of environmental information is that from the
Office of Science and Technology, the operating office headed by
the Science Advisor to the President of the United States. These
are policy-type documents relating, for example, to energy and the
environment. From the standpoint of origin and content, one might
say they closely parallel the Council for Environmental Quality.

This office has published reports bearing such titles as:

Protecting the World Environment in the Light of
Population Increase (December 1970)

Cumulative Regulatory Effects on the Cost of Automotive
    Transportation (RECAT)   (February 28, 1972)

The Universities and Environmental Quality (September 1969)

Electric Power and the Environment (October 1970)

NATIONAL INDUSTRIAL POLLUTION CONTROL COUNCIL

The sixth category of environmental information is that from the
National Industrial Pollution Control Council. This Council, created
by Executive Order 11523 on April 9, 1970, is a constituent oper-
ating unit of the Department of Commerce, a lesser creature in the
Commerce hierarchy which includes the Patent Office and NTIS.
The Council staff is under the Assistant Secretary for Economic
Affairs; the Council members are industrial executives, usually cor-
poration presidents.

The makeup and functions of the Council are reported in a Council
Report dated February 1971. A Sub-Council report on "The
Chemical Industry and Pollution Control" was issued in June 1971.

The Council publications are usually short (20 to 50 pages) in length
and do not give much technical detail.

THE NATIONAL ACADEMY OF SCIENCES - NATIONAL RESEARCH COUNCIL

The seventh category of environmental information to be discussed
here is that available from the Printing and Publishing Office of the
National Academy of Sciences at 2101 Constitution Avenue in
Washington. These are usually the results of panel studies of various
environmental problems and they bear such titles as:

"Impact of Air Pollution Regulations on Fuel Selection
    for Federal Facilities"

"Jamaica Bay and Kennedy Airport: A Multidisciplinary
    Environmental Study"

"Waste Management Concepts for the Coastal Zone".

THE CONGRESS

The eighth category of environmental information to be discussed here includes the publications of the Congress of the United States.

These publications usually result from hearings on various types of environmental legislation. They are available most promptly and free of charge from the committee which issues them. Learning of their availability at an early date is the trick. One way of learning is by examining the listing of "Printed Hearings and Documents" in each Friday's issue of the Congressional Monitor, published in Washington by Robert Townsend at a subscription price of $285 per year.

A typical recent example is "Mercury Pollution and Enforcement of the Refuse Act of 1899," being a 1089 page print of Hearings Before the Subcommittee on Conservation and Natural Resources of the Committee on Government Operations of the House of Representatives (July 1971). Among its contents are the entire text of a Sierra Club "Battlebook on Mercury" which normally retails at $2.25. The whole volume of hearings is available free from the Committee or for $4.50 from the Superintendent of Documents, United States Government Printing Office.

BIBLIOGRAPHIC SOURCES

The ninth category of environmental information to be considered here is the bibliographic publications.

In this category, one private corporation, the Output Systems Corporation of Arlington, Virginia is publishing an annual reference volume which covers (in its first volume) the pollution aspects of air, water, radiation, solid wastes and pesticides including the categories of:

(1) organization and function of federal agencies;
(2) names, addresses and phone numbers of federal and
        state officials;
(3) standards and criteria;
(4) agency budgets;
(5) individual program descriptions.

Further, in the bibliographic area, we have publications such as the listing of Government publications on air, water and land pollution, 1965-70, prepared by the Institute of Public Affairs of Western Michigan University and "Man and His Environment -- Selected Government Publications 1950-1970" prepared by the Government Publications Department of the Indiana University Library (April 1970).

Also, a computerized directory of information centers, research projects and individual investigators has been established by the NSF-supported Environmental Information Program at Oak Ridge National Laboratory to serve research administrators, scientists and information specialists who wish to contact active workers in the environmental field.

In addition, the Woodrow Wilson International Center for Scholars at the Smithsonian Institute in Washington, D.C. has just issued "The Human Environment" in two volumes. Volume I is a selected annotated bibliography on international aspects of environmental control and Volume II consists of summaries of national reports presented at Stockholm in 1972.

REVIEW PUBLICATIONS

The tenth and final category of sources of environmental information to be considered here are the review publications which draw on all the various sources cited previously in this paper.

The author of this paper essayed two such publications, one on air pollution control in 1968 and one on water pollution control and solid waste disposal in 1969. These are both out of print.

Now, several publications have issued from Noyes Data Corporation, Park Ridge, New Jersey, largely based on information from patents and various Government reports. These cover mercury pollution control, sulfuric acid plant effluent control, detergents and pollution, particulate pollution and pollution in various specific industry categories. They are listed in the attached table.

CONCLUSION

In conclusion, then, a wealth of information on environmental pollution, its measurement and control exists in a variety of Government publications. In this paper an attempt has been made to spell out the routes to such information and to collections of such information.

I hope it has been helpful and useful to you.

NDC Environmental Books Based on Government Sources

Gutcho, S., "Waste Treatment with Polyelectrolytes" (1972).
Jones, H.R., "Mercury Pollution Control" (1971).
Jones, H.R., "Environmental Control in the Inorganic Chemical Industry" (1972).
Jones, H.R., "Environmental Control in the Organic and Petrochemical Industries" (1972).
Jones, H.R., "Detergents and Pollution -- Problems and Technological Solutions" (1972).
Jones, H.R., "Fine Dust and Particulates Removal" (1972).
McDermott, J., "Catalytic Conversion of Automobile Exhaust" (1971).
McDonald, M., "Paper Recycling and the Use of Chemicals" (1971).
Sittig, M., "Sulfuric Acid Manufacture & Effluent Control" (1971).
Slack, A.V., "Sulfur Dioxide Removal from Waste Gases" (1971).
Stecher, P.G., "Hydrogen Sulfide Removal Processes" (1972).
AIChE, "Complying with Sulfur Dioxide Regulations" (1972).
Post, D., "Noncatalytic Auto Exhaust Reduction" (1972).
Lawrence, A.A., "Nitrogen Oxides Emission Control" (1972).
James, R.W., "Sewage Sludge Treatment" (1972).
Jones, H.R., "Pollution Control in the Nonferrous Metals Industry" (1972).
Jones, H.R., "Waste Control in the Fruit and Vegetable Processing Industry" (1972).
Jones, H.R., "Pollution Control in the Textile Industry" (in press).
Jones, H.R., "Pollution Control in the Pulp and Paper Industry" (in press).

SORTING IT OUT

DATA VS. INFORMATION

Steven S. Ross
Editor, NEW ENGINEER

I'd like to explore some techniques for turning incoming environmental data into information that may be acted upon with some confidence. The idea is not to build up an internal data bank. In this area, we have libraries that do a fair job, but for the latest news of new products and for judging the "climate" of current markets and enforcement, you must act on your own. However, even before going to a library to track down a piece of information, it helps to have at least a hazy idea of what is worthwhile to look for.

At first glance, there is no shortage of information on environmental matters. In addition to the strictly environmental publications listed in the bibliography, there are symposia, conferences and myriad Government publications, many quite good and all quite cheap. Most publications catering to chemists and chemical engineers, including Chemical Engineering, with which I was formerly associated, have found wide reader interest in environmental articles. What keeps the reader happy, keeps advertisers happy. What keeps advertisers happy, keeps publishers happy. Therefore, on the order of a third to a fourth of all articles written in the trade press last year have something to do with environmental problems.

The question for you then, is, "Are these articles the ones I need? Am I getting the information I want, as early as needed,with no misinformation? Am I paying as low a price as possible, both in reading and conference attending time, and in subscription costs?" The answer to these questions for most of you is probably, "No." There is, in fact, a great deal of misinformation being published on environmental matters these days. Much of the data derives from the same source. Some is irrelevant to specific branches of our field; some irrelevant to everybody. Sometimes the nuggets of information are imbedded in a rich vein of trivia and misstatement.

I'd like then today to give you some guidelines on how to seek the information buried in that mountain of environmental data that crosses the desks of so many of you every week. To do that, I'd first like to give you a crash course in the publications business, its strengths and limitations. I'd then like to discuss some specific examples, some horror stories, if you like, and by doing that, point out that an information source good for one person may be marginal, or even useless, to a colleague.

Some basics: Publications and other information sources come in all sizes, shapes and colors. There are magazines; those aimed broadly at the chemical field, those aimed specifically at environmental affairs. There are technical journals; some supported by page charges to the author, some by stiff fees for subscriptions, some by the professional society that publishes them. Some, including the Water Pollution Control Federation's monthly Journal, carry advertising to help defray expenses.

There are newsletters, usually weekly, or biweekly, usually devoid of ads, carrying fancy price tags. There are binder services, in which looseleaf reference data is continually updated, sometimes on a regular basis, but more often irregularly, with new pages that the reader (more often the reader's secretary if there is one) files in the binder. There are also newspapers, some of which do a rather good job of following events in our field.

Where does the money to do this come from? In publications that carry advertising, most of the money comes from the ads. In fact, sometimes all the money comes from ads; many environmental publications come to you absolutely free.

At the very least, a magazine will write stories that are designed to be read by the audience the advertiser wants to reach. That can work to your benefit. At the very worst, advertisers in a few publications will dictate how a story will be written, i.e., what companies and products to play up in the story, and what potentially embarrassing facts to ignore about the company's products. There is an in-between. Sometimes a story is written in such a way as to satisfy the reader without telling him anything worthwhile. Thus some environmental publications on shaky financial ground are blatantly pro-industry. It's nice to feel loved, but perhaps we have some faults worth correcting, faults we might correct if the magazine would tell us about them before the pollution control officer or local newspaper does.

The cost of publications that do not carry advertising is often quite steep. Air and Water News, a weekly newsletter I edited until a few months ago, cost $145 a year. Bureau of National Affairs sells Environment Reporter, a binder service for $340 a year.

Next, publications do not write themselves. The writing is done by reporters and editors. Naturally, these reporters and editors (and that includes me) all have their biases, blind spots and hangups.

The obvious biases are usually easy to spot. More difficult to follow, however, are the less obvious biases and special interests of the writer or editor. Just as different chemists are interested in different areas of chemistry and chemical engineering, so too are different writers interested in different pieces of the whole environmental story. You may find the publication you want, just the publication you need. You get used to it and then the key writer leaves. Suggestion number one: When you find a writer whose interests match yours, follow him. Often he's been enticed away to another publication. How do you find out which one? Simple. Call the publication you've been reading and ask where the writer went. Don't say why you want to know.

There is another aspect of information dispersion that is almost axiomatic: The amount of exposure a piece of information receives is directly proportional to the degree of success being described, and increases geometrically according to the finances of the disseminating organization. In plain English, companies rarely invest in a press release to describe their failures. But large firms can afford to bury editors with releases for so-called "successes" that may be marginal or even trivial.

So, then, how does a magazine find out about failures? By keeping its eyes open, and spending money, sometimes a lot of money, on digging out the facts itself. Clearly the professional will have to spend more time finding out about failures than about successes. So look at the size of the editorial staff. It takes only one man to cut and paste press releases.

What about lead time? How old is the data when you get it? Books and professional journals are perhaps the worst offenders in this regard; delays of a year or more are not uncommon. But the journals are usually pretty honest about this. Down at the foot of the first page, you'll often see the date the paper was written, or first presented for publication.

On the other hand, journals are not very good about telling what the strengths of their editorial staff are. Seemingly impressive mastheads often list mainly consulting editors, editorial boards, or editors serving several publications at once. For instance, a quarterly journal I'm familiar with carried the names of dozens of experts in the field who referred papers, i.e., decided which papers were suitable for publication. After that, all editorial changes, layout approvals, necessary drafting problems, proofreading, and most author correspondence was done by an editorial assistant. I was that editorial assistant, working part time as a college senior. This situation is more the rule than the exception on journals.

Trade magazines usually have more staff, but their lead times can be deceiving. The feature articles in a typical monthly are written three months before the date of issue. Most monthlies try to keep some space open for last minute news and changes, but even then, such news is usually at least two weeks, and often six weeks late in getting to the reader.

Newsletters can do better as far as time is concerned. Since they are usually composed on an electric typewriter and produced photo-offset, last-minute corrections can often be made scant hours before a newsletter is in the mail to the readers.

Of course, the publications with the shortest lead times are the newspapers. A story written late Monday night can be replicated a millionfold by Tuesday morning, and updated the very next day, if need be.

Now, there is a law of publication dynamics. In theory, the longer the lead time, the more insightful, well thought out, and the better written is the article. It follows, therefore, that speed isn't everything. Do you have to spend a premium in time plowing through a newspaper or the Federal Register for your news, or a premium in money with a subscription to a costly newsletter? Or will three months' delay be okay? Will it be okay for somethings, but not for others?

Are you most interested in the "letter of the law" as it affects your businesses, or are you more interested in the environmental "climate" without the specifics? Perhaps you or your firms want to comment to the Federal Environmental Protection Agency on proposed regulations before those regulations appear in final form etched into the pages of the Federal Register.

For Federal regulations, this is easy. The proposed rule-making, along with the time limits for comments and the address to which comments should be sent, also appears in the Federal Register. The modest investment of $25 a year, tax deductible, brings this paragon of information to you five times a week. Since that is so easy, and the topic of Government environmental documents has been pre-empted, I'll pose a more difficult question: What about advance word of proposed rule-making in the States?

If I may digress, this is a constant complaint of mine. Most State pollution officers are happy to put companies on their mailing lists for news of upcoming hearings and proposed rule-making, free, no less. But most companies don't want to contact State officials. I spoke in December to a crowd of 300 industry people at the Plaza, beginning my speech by asking how many had spoken or written to a State pollution control official recently. Fewer than a dozen hands went up.

Members of the audience came up after the talk and generally said that telling them to contact State officials was easy for me to say. But no one wants to open a can of worms. Well, gentlemen, contrary to what you read in the newspapers and most of the trade press, most pollution control officials are indeed human. They don't have horns. Those horror stories you read about are news precisely because they are horror stories. Considering especially that your only outside source of information on State happenings is the local paper, you must go after State news yourself.

Now, to get back on the track and talk about outside information sources. Suppose you've reviewed your own particular needs for environmental information. Armed with the short course in the publications business, how do you go about getting what you need? What pitfalls should you avoid?

First, view promotional literature for publications, especially expensive ones such as newsletters and binder services, with an analytical eye. They all tell you about the fantastic staff of experts combing the halls of Washington and reading hundreds of journals for you. Promotion pieces tell of concise and cogent prose, unerringly accurate and timely. Well, given the constraints of skill and money no publication can be all things to all people. One way to find out whether a publication covers what you are interested in is to take a trial subscription. Most magazines and newsletters will give you a few weeks free, or even a few months at a nominal cost. Take them up on their offers and read them critically.

Second, avoid the temptation to buy a broad spectrum news service unless you absolutely need it. They cost more, take longer to read, and make you pay also for information of little or no value to you.

Third, pay only for the timeliness you really need. For instance, Air and Water News was usually a week ahead of the Federal Register in publishing major environmental regulations. The extra effort necessary to be ahead of the pack costs money which was reflected in higher than typical subscription costs, even for a newsletter. Unless you need the information ahead of time, you might be wasting money.

Fourth, constantly review your portfolio of publication subscriptions, as your needs change, as the environmental situation changes, and as the publications themselves, many of them quite new, evolve. For instance to my mind, the biggest environmental stories now revolve around the theme: "What are the Feds up to now?" I have hopes that by this time next year most of the rule-making will be done, and enforcement will be standardized across the country. The big story then for most of us will be: "Now that we know what the Feds want us to do, how will we do it?"

So for many of you, consultants especially, a good newsletter can be a useful ally now to get the latest out of Washington. But the importance of newsletters could decline for many people within the next year or two, as the story emphasis moves from Washington to technical matters.

I'd like now to get down to some specifics, some recommendations as to what publications are most useful for particular purposes. The recommendations are highly personal and colored by my own experience. Publications I mention have either been of great use to me in covering this whole broad field of environmental issues, or have come up with enterprising coverage of specific facets of this field. Some of my choices may surprise you.

For coverage of the general environmental mood in Washington, my seal of approval goes to E.W. Kenworthy of The New York Times, and the news staff of Science Magazine. The Times can be quite superficial, given the constraints of its tight daily deadlines and orientation toward happenings that affect the average reader. For instance, its report of the final version of the 1970 Clean Air Amendments dealt almost exclusively with the provisions calling for a 90% reduction in automobile emissions by 1975. On the other hand, Kenworthy receives many tips from environmental groups and disgruntled bureaucrats.

Almost every issue of Science carries an overview of some environmental law or regulation. The reporting is often not as timely as it might be, but it is generally accurate, and touches on some items, such as the mercury in fish imbroglio, with a broad view that is hard to match in the more specialized trade magazines, and with a depth and sophistication impossible in newspapers.

There are several publications useful for nationwide environmental coverage.

Corporate lawyers, enforcement officials and environmental lawyers can hardly do without the Bureau of National Affairs' Environment Reporter. This is a binder service which continually updates Federal and State laws, publishes environmental court decisions, and supplies a 20-page environmental overview each week. Environment Reporter does not spend as much time as it might, however, in recognizing and covering technical news and it rarely tries to interpret or place into perspective environmental happenings. This, along with its bulk, often makes it of limited value for busy executives.

A quite different publication that concentrates more on technical articles is Environment Information Access, a biweekly service which abstracts 1,100 publications, including everything from newspapers to technical journals and patents. Access has republication agreements with many journals, for which it can provide copies of complete articles for a modest fee. The abstracts themselves cost $150 per year. They are well cross-indexed by computer, with an annual index also available. I find Access quick and easy to use, an important consideration when doing a literature search. Look for it in libraries if you can't justify the cost of a subscription for your purposes. Of course, Chemical Abstracts may be found there too.

Managers and plant engineers in the chemical industry most often cite Plant Engineering and Chemical Engineering as carrying the most useful environmental information for them. To them, I would add Environmental Science and Technology. Unfortunately, this ACS publication is a monthly with a longer-than-optimal lead time for the fast-moving environmental field.

Consultants and engineers for larger, more diverse companies should also be getting a host of technical journals. Topping the list for those mainly interested in water pollution is the monthly Journal of the Water Pollution Control Federation. The Journal has in the past been too slow in getting papers into print, but it has greatly improved under new editorial direction. Take a look if you haven't seen it lately. Federation members also get a monthly bulletin into which is folded "Deeds and Data," chock full of actual case histories of plant problems and solutions. The bias is toward municipal situations. Engineers designing plants for municipalities, please take note.

Another monthly, the Air Pollution Control Association Journal, has traces of genius. However, some Federal enforcement officials complain that the journal has an anti-EPA bias in its Washington column.

I have found the whole range of ASCE publications useful in covering subjects of general concern to consultants, especially in catching such nuances as changes in where to find money for environmental projects.

Consider these journals the bare minimum for keeping ahead of the competition which is most likely also reading them. For the latest information on changing or new technologies, make a serious effort to scan advertising in all the trade books you get. Build up a file of company literature. This is easy with the readership service cards now bound into just about every magazine that comes your way. Circle the number corresponding to the literature you want, and pop the card into the mail.

Suppose you are the owner of a small plant who has just been told to control your pollution, "or else." Suppose you take the pollution control officer seriously. Where do you go to get environmental help? Many publications publish an environmental directory issue once a year or so. Among the best are the "Environmental Engineering Deskbook" published by Chemical Engineering annually in the late spring. Environmental Science and Technology devotes a fall issue to a directory, too.

Perhaps the best lists of environmental consultants come free to

members of the Water Pollution Control Federation and the Air
Pollution Control Association. The best listing of companies that
provide effluent and emission testing services is ASTM's publication
333B, which costs $3.50. Noyes Data lists 1,500 suppliers of envi-
ronmental services and products in "Pollution Control Companies
USA" which costs $24. Interestingly, all these listings have com-
panies included that no one else has. But frankly, having any one
or two of these books on your desk should do the trick.

I'm sure that many of you know that legislation pending in Congress
calls for premarket clearance of a broad range of chemicals, and a
review of the environmental safety of products already on the market. The scramble has only just begun to assemble toxicity data on
existing chemical products and classes of chemicals into which new
products may fall. Some trade associations, such as the Dry Color
Manufacturers' Association, are helping gather such information for
their members. If you are in a field of chemistry where toxicity,
and, I might add, possible genetic effects of your product or proposed products may be questionable, start getting your hands on
such data now.

One place to look is "Abstracts on Health Effects of Environmental
Pollutants," selected by BioSciences Information Service from Biosis
and Medlars. Another place is the Environmental Mutagen Information Center of the Oak Ridge National Laboratory.

There is one area of environmental data-gathering where I can offer
no advice except caution: Marketing reports on environmental products. Considering the fancy price tags most of them carry, their
quality is atrocious. Perhaps the reasons for this are simple. The
environmental marketplace over the past few years has been changing quickly and dramatically. Data are often out of date and misleading, even as they are being written into the market study. But
after all, a writer of such a study can't afford to say he is unsure of
a piece of information. People paying $500 to $5,000 for a marketing report want it chiseled in stone. That kind of money should buy
unerring truth and perfection!

I am asked almost daily to provide figures for this or that segment
of the environmental market. The conversion often begins with me
saying that I have the figures, but that they are wrong, or aren't important figures in the first place. Such conversations often end with
me giving the figures anyway, after much begging on the other end
of the line.

In summary: No matter what those promotional brochures say, there is probably no one environmental information source completely right for you. And the best source may not be an "environmental" publication at all, but rather continuing environmental coverage by a trade magazine or journal, or even a newspaper.

A strong data base today usually starts with Government information, especially the Federal Register. However, for interpretation, writers who are governed by the laws of economics are a necessity. Also, you should not be afraid to reach out for personal contact with environmental officials yourselves. Especially in this part of the country, there are many who are knowledgeable and willing to help. Do not use them, however, as a substitute for a reputable consultant or consulting firm which has presumably spent some time and money sorting out all the environmental data to produce salable and useful information.

And when all else fails in this chaotic field, pray! Thank you.

SELECTED LIST OF ENVIRONMENTAL PUBLICATIONS

As almost all trade magazines and journals publish environmental articles, this list is restricted to those publications which (1) devote all of their space to environmental issues, and (2) are especially useful to the chemical field.

Abstracting Services

> Abstracts on Health Effects of Environmental Pollutants
> Biosciences Information Service
> 2100 Arch Street
> Philadelphia, Pa. 19103
>> $95 for 12 monthly issues. Selected material from Medlars and Biosis.

> Environment Information Access
> Environment Information Center
> 124 E. 39th Street
> New York, N.Y. 10016
>> $150 for 24 twice monthly issues. Abstracts 1,100 publications. Annual index, keyed to abstracts, available for $75.

Pollution Abstracts
P.O. Box 2369
La Jolla, Calif. 92037
   $70 for six bimonthly issues.

Binder Services

Environment Reporter
Bureau of National Affairs, Inc.
1231 25th St. N.W.,
Washington, D.C. 20037
   $340 a year, updated weekly.

DMS Environmental Services
DMS Market Intelligence Reports
100 Northfield Street
Greenwich, Conn. 06830
   Updated irregularly.

Newsletters

Air and Water News
Trends Publishing
801 New Center Bldg.
Detroit, Mich. 48202
   $145 for 52 weekly issues.

Air/Water Pollution Report
Business Publishers, Inc.
P.O. Box 1067, Blair Station,
Silver Spring, Md. 20910
   $120 for 52 weekly issues. Same company publishes
   a solid wastes newsletter.

Clean Air and Water News
Commerce Clearinghouse
4025 W. Peterson Avenue
Chicago, Ill. 60646

ChemEcology
Manufacturing Chemists Association
1825 Connecticut Avenue N.W.
Washington, D.C. 20009
   Continues Currents and Pilot. MCA also can supply

lists of state legislation passed and pending.

Environmental Control News for Southern Industry
Monthly from Enviro-Trol,
P.O. Box 4131
Memphis, Tenn. 38104

Journals

Air Pollution Control Association
4400 Fifth Avenue
Pittsburgh, Pa. 15213
    $25 for 12 monthly issues.

Water Pollution Control Federation
3900 Wisconsin Avenue
Washington, D.C. 20016
    $15 for 12 monthly issues.

American Water Works Association
2 Park Avenue
New York, N.Y. 10016
    $15 for 12 monthly issues.

(Contact the author for information on literally hundreds of additional journals, concentrating more on environmental effects than on control technology.)

Magazines

Environmental Science and Technology
American Chemical Society
1155 Sixteenth Street N.W.
Washington, D.C. 20036
    $9 for non-ACS members, for 12 monthly issues.
    Includes "magazine" with general review and technical articles, with a back "journal" section.

Industrial Wastes
Scranton Publishing Co.
35 E. Wacker Drive
Chicago, Ill. 60601
    Bimonthly.

Industrial Water Engineering
Target Communications
373 Fifth Avenue
New York, N.Y. 10016
  Monthly.

Pollution Engineering
Technical Publishing Co.
35 Mason Street
Greenwich, Conn. 06830
  Bimonthly.

Pollution Equipment News
Richard Rimbach
8550 Babcock Blvd.
Pittsburgh, Pa. 15237

Water & Sewage Works
Scranton Publishing
35 E. Wacker Drive
Chicago, Ill. 60601
  Monthly.

Water and Wastes Engineering
Reuben Donnelley Corp.
466 Lexington Avenue
New York, N.Y. 10017
  Bimonthly.

Environmental Control & Safety Management
A.M. Best Co.
Park Avenue
Morristown, N.J. 07960
  Monthly.

Directories

Names and addresses of firms supplying environmental services are
listed in special issues of the Air Pollution Control Association,
Water Pollution Control Federation, Public Works, Chemical
Engineering, Environmental Science and Technology. In addition
the publications listed on the following page give similar information.

"Pollution Control Companies U.S.A."
Noyes Data Corp.
Park Ridge, N.J. 07656
   $24

"ASTM Directory of Testing Labs"
American Society for Testing and Materials
1916 Race Street
Philadelphia, Pa.
   $3.50

"Your Government and the Environment"
Output Systems
P.O. Box 2407
Arlington, Va. 22202

"Monthly Catalog of U.S. Gov't. Publications"
USGPO
Washington, D.C. 20402
   $7 per year.

QUESTION PERIOD FOLLOWING MR. ROSS'S PRESENTATION

Dr. Schildknecht: You implied a chaotic state of publishing these days, and I wonder if you could comment about the current policy of publishing a fast magazine supported by advertising. It is only natural that a few things which are published are not true. I'm not blaming the publishers, but if you are going to operate under these circumstances and be paid by the advertising, you have got to gather quickly some scientific material to put between the advertising to make the magazine.

What is your policy about answering the mail of your critics? Do you make your files available, for example, in patent matters? If you publish some misinformation and the person using it has a patent that depends on it, and he writes to you, is it your policy to answer all such mail? Is it your policy ever to make your files available for scientific or technical reasons?

Mr. Ross: Speaking for myself, the policy on Air and Water News and Chemical Engineering was to correct mistakes as soon as possible because a great deal of money sometimes is riding on those pages, on those things you print. The policy also is to answer letters as soon as possible.

The publications change very fast. <u>Air and Water News</u>, for instance, grew out of <u>Chemical Engineering</u> in 1966 along with three or four environmental publications. Now there are, according to the last count, something in the order of 100 or 110 devoted to environmental health.

<u>Environmental Information Access</u> abstracts 1,100 journals, many of them health journals in the environmental field. To give you an idea of what you are up against, Engineering Societies Library has gathered two or three thousand publications and environmental publication articles in the past year or so alone. <u>Access</u> has 47,000 articles in the data bank. <u>Pollution Abstracts</u> has even more. There is just a huge amount of information; a huge amount of data coming out. You have to decide for yourselves by reviewing these publications as to their worth. Send in for a trial subscription. Send in the card. Many of them are free. Check on them yourselves. That is the best possible advice I can give you.

Henry Friedlander (Union Carbide): Most of the discussion implies that we are talking about the macrocosm, the big industry, government, and so forth.

Do you have any good sources of information regarding what the homeowner may think, for example, about odor control, or water tasting bad — the microcosm. What about the individual consumer in shifting thoughts that are meaningful and perhaps economic?

Mr. Ross: One good publication for this purpose is <u>Consumer Reports</u> and its like. The Federal Trade Commission publishes a newsletter that costs a dollar a year covering many of these topics. Just the last issue, for instance, contained a piece concerned with lead and other heavy metals paints and with possible regulations for reactive hydrocarbon solvents in paints you might use around the house. It pointed out that in some cases they might be illegal. It covered very well the battle of which you may know very well. EPA in its original standards wanted paints with certain solvents to come only in quart size containers or smaller. It was finally decided by "the powers that be" that this really wasn't necessary, since it was such a small contribution, really, to the total pollution load as to be insignificant.

I would say on the household level, let's face it, that a great deal of the information disseminated is highly speculative and poorly put together; basically wrong. I think a good example of this was the dispute over the phosphates. It is happening now with leaded gasoline. There are technical arguments on both sides, but they are being picked up from the wrong end. The meaning of these controversies to their audience, their homeowner reader who may or may not have adequate sewage treatment, who may or may not be using a septic tank, who may or may not be using electric heat, who may or may not have public transportation, is not covered.

Consequently we are seeing more and more technical people; college professors, plant managers, plant engineers, and so forth, becoming columnists for their own local papers because the ordinary reporters aren't doing the job.

Moderator Tuwiner: It has been my observation on the subject of accuracy that announcements of new processes are almost invariably accurate; cost estimates that are made, including those in many respectable journals and Government publications, are generally inaccurate and almost invariably not conservative. I wonder how, in view of this fact that people don't blush to be estimating about 50% low on the process. I wonder what thought you might have on that.

Mr. Ross: There are two schools of thought on this. One is that you have someone who has come up with a new process. He is giving a figure which you are bound to report, citing the source. Hopefully you can find some disclaimer.

The other school of thought says, "Don't put in the cost figures at all." Very often though, when we are reporting new things, new sources, questions do come up. For example, if you have a new process, is it more economical; is it better than what exists now; does it cause another problem you can't solve; and what is being taken into the cost equation? I know that in Air and Water News we got eighty news releases a day, and on the order of only three or four of these a week would form the basis for articles.

"Unique" is the most overworked word in the news release writer's dictionary. What we at Chemical Engineering attempted to do is estimate the cost ourselves, or carefully spell out that this is a pilot project stage or semiscale, or that this is just a gleam in some professor's eye.

The general editorial philosophy for most respectable publications is to say that the closer a project is to commercialization the more accurate its cost figures will be, or can be assumed to be. It is hard for a reporter to judge. I think the only way he can really judge is by some method of personal experience. Be very careful to find out what assumptions are being made on the basis of base cost figures, i.e., what are the cost figures based on. If the energy needed for the process is given, you can estimate it if you have some familiarity with the equipment. A reasonable estimate might be plus or minus 30 or 40%

Moderator Tuwiner: Just by way of taking the privilege of the Chairman to make one final comment, I think that in former years, when publications were generally looked upon as something more substantial and lasting because people continued to refer to them for many years, some of the things that went into them went in with a great deal more sense of responsibility than is the case today where for the most part publications are read and then thrown out. We have the same viewpoint toward them as we would towards something we might read in the daily papers, so that this seems to have some effect on the people who write the material for them. They don't write for posterity, and the thought doesn't occur to them that what they say may in a few years look pretty silly because they know very well all of it by that time will have been forgotten.

ENVIRONMENTAL CONTROL RESOURCES
OF A LARGE TECHNICAL LIBRARY

Kirk Cabeen
Director, Engineering Societies Library

This discussion concerns the resources of the Engineering Societies Library as they relate specifically to environmental control. I will start with a brief history of the Library, show its relationship to the twelve societies which help support it, describe the services available from it, spend some time talking about Engineering Index and its services, discuss some of the environmental control tools available at the Library, and finally try to give you some pointers on how to conduct a literature search to uncover already published information on the specific area of environmental control in which you might be currently interested.

The Engineering Societies Library was officially founded in 1913, but had its beginnings earlier in this century when the then American Institute of Electrical Engineers, the American Society of Mechanical Engineers and the American Institute of Mining Engineers decided to combine their libraries and move under one roof. They approached Andrew Carnegie, who offered to build them a communal headquarters, the old engineering societies building on West 39th Street.

They were later joined by the American Society of Civil Engineers and later still by the American Institute of Chemical Engineers. These five societies formed a corporation called United Engineering Trustees, Inc. which owns the Engineering Societies Library and the headquarters building.

A new building was completed in 1961 on 47th Street at the corner of First Avenue. This building houses not only the Library and the

so-called Founder Societies but also other engineering societies who
rent space in the building and help support the Library. Other independent organizations in the building include Engineering Index, Inc.,
Engineers Joint Council, Engineering Foundation and Welding Research
Council.

The Engineering Societies Library which has now grown to be the
largest library in the world devoted exclusively to engineering and
applied technology, is governed by a Board of chosen representatives
of the Founder and Associate Societies. It has a staff of 40 employees, 16 of whom are professional librarians. It is open to the public,
though only members of supporting societies may borrow books. It
provides all the services of other public libraries and has in addition
a literature searching and translating department. We can supply
photocopy or microfilm of any article in the collection.

An independent corporation located adjacent to the Library is
Engineering Index. All the technical journals, unpublished papers
and symposia proceedings received in the Library are made available
to Engineering Index which selectively abstracts and indexes them.
These abstracts are published in various forms on a subscription basis.

Card-A-Lert provides weekly mailings in specific subject categories.
There are, for example, categories for air pollution, waste treatment,
and water pollution. Another form of publication is the Monthly
Bulletin which covers all abstracts prepared that month arranged by
subject with an author index. These Monthly Bulletins are cumulated into the "EI Annual." The abstracts are also issued on magnetic tape and sent to subscribers monthly. This service is called
Compendex.

Last year EI produced over 85,000 abstracts. Of these, 900 dealt
with air pollution, 625 with waste treatment, 600 with water pollution. A significant advantage of the working relationship between
the Library and the Index is that hard copy of any article covered
by the Engineering Index can be procured from the Engineering
Societies Library.

Though the subject of environmental control has fairly recently come
into national and international prominence, it is far from a new concept, and there is a considerable amount of open literature on the
subject. In the last 20 years and especially within the last five, new
periodicals and new indexing services have sprung up like weeds.
(Some of them are little better than weeds, too, but I am not here

to make value judgments on someone else's product.) Even before the 1950's, however, a wealth of material on air pollution, water supply, industrial waste treatment and other aspects of environmental control were talked about and written about. A technical research library like the ESL has this historical material as well as current references on file, indexed and easily available to the researcher.

Our subject card catalog has, for example, over 2,500 index cards to specific books, symposia and pamphlets dealing with air and water pollution. You may rightly protest that you don't want to look at 2,500 cards, let alone 2,500 books. The chances are, of course, that you are interested in only a particular aspect of air or water pollution, and our catalog provides many sub-headings under these two broad terms which will let you be much more specific in selecting material.

If you are, in fact, embarking on a literature search, the first thing to do is to go where the literature is — i.e. a large technical library. The place to begin a search is not with a subject card catalog or an abstracting service, but with bibliographies of your subject. If you can locate a recent and thoroughly published bibliography, the searching part of your job may already be done.

The bibliography section on air pollution of the ESL catalog has 68 references to published bibliographies. Not all are current, some deal with limited or specific aspects, and some are far from extensive, but as a jumping-off place, published bibliographies are the best spot to use. You may well find enough references to pertinent material to satisfy your needs. If not, your next step should be the subject card catalog. From there proceed to periodical indexing and abstracting services such as Engineering Index, Pollution Abstracts, or other specialized services whose existence you will have learned about from the card catalog. For the very latest material you will need to use a current awareness tool such as Environmental Periodicals which reproduces the Tables of Contents pages from recent journals.

To accomplish a literature search you must be prepared to spend time, either yours or someone else's. Barring the existence of a good up-to-date published bibliography which is right on your topic, the literature search staff at the Engineering Societies Library generally estimate that a preliminary search on a subject will require 10 to 20 hours to perform. Exhaustive searches, of course, can take considerably longer.

This has been a very quick overview of the Engineering Societies Library, its makeup and resources, some of its services, and its relationship to Engineering Index. If you have an environmental control problem connected with your job, I invite you to come, call or write to the Library and we will do the best we can to help you.

QUESTION PERIOD FOLLOWING MR. CABEEN'S PRESENTATION

Henry Friedlander (Union Carbide): Would you comment on the extent of your Government reports, particularly EPA reports of which there are hundreds and thousands?

Mr. Cabeen: We are not a repository for Government documents. We collect them on a selective basis. Our acquisitions librarian goes through the Government catalog and selects only those that he feels are germane to engineering and applied technology. We probably have most of them, I would say. I believe the New York Public Library is a complete depository for Government documents, so they would have them all.

Dr. Schildknecht: To what extent do you have Russian and Japanese?

Mr. Cabeen: I am not sure just how much the Russians, Japanese and Chinese have been doing in the area of environmental control, so I hesitate to say what environmental material we might have on those subjects. We collect fairly extensively in the Russian language, quite limitedly in Japanese and nothing in Chinese because we haven't been able to get it. The problem with the Oriental languages is very few people can read them, and unless there is an English abstract that goes with them nobody knows what they are about. There is nobody in Engineering Index who can translate Japanese, so they will take a Japanese article if it has an English abstract with it.

I might say most Japanese articles do come with an English abstract. And, of course, many of the publications are translated cover to cover.

Mr. Sittig (Princeton University): Would you identify the publisher of the new periodical mentioned in your discussion.

Mr. Cabeen: Environmental Periodicals is published by Environmental

Studies Institute, International Academy at Santa Barbara, Sierra Campus, 2048 Alameda, Padre Sierra, Santa Barbara, Calif. 93103. The price per volume is $55. These are advertised in the "Annual Index" for $65. It is going to be published eight times a year, with the ninth issue in December containing the annual index — or maybe that will be the annual index.

Question: What were the three categories you referred to?

Mr. Cabeen: They are Air Pollution, Water Treatment, and Water Pollution. These are the three categories published by Engineering Index. The Library is not involved in these publications. The prices are either $50 or $75 depending on the amount of material that has come out over the last year. Water Pollution is $50, Air Pollution is $75.

PANEL DISCUSSION

Sidney B. Tuwiner, Ph.D.
Moderator

Moderator Tuwiner: Let us have Dr. Conrad address some comments to one of the speakers, and then have the speaker respond.

Dr. Carleton C. Conrad (Manager, Central Report Index): I have been listening here to some excellent speakers, people who spend their time, most of their time, or a good portion of their time in the field of environmental activities and information. I look upon my own program as somewhat more restricted. I think I am on this program to supply a balance, as it were, between outside activity with what is very much a proprietary activity.

I am involved with the Du Pont Research Reporting Activity. Inside Du Pont we have a retrieval system for proprietary Du Pont research information.

We also have an internal activity for patent information. We have an internal centralized activity for contact with Government sources. We do have a program for contact with the environmental area, particularly since so many things have been happening recently that this has become a very active area in which Government regulations are promulgated for industry compliance. Not only are products that you sell on the market involved, but your very operations, as has been pointed out, are involved.

I was very interested today because you cannot talk about your own research activity without saying what effect the research operation that we are talking about or are interested in will have on the environment. And we are often called upon internally to supply information as to what we know internally about contaminants, about purity, about the whole area that has been presented to us so far today.

I was interested particularly in a very interesting conversation I had this morning with Mr. Ross. I was very stimulated by what he had to say and I will address my remarks to Mr. Ross.

I was interested in some comments that he made regarding news-letters, particularly the comment regarding the value of information with respect to its timeliness, i.e., the more timely it seems to be the less reliable it may be in some regard. And concerning the fact that retrospective files of information for which our Library here is a famous source, and which we all need to consult from time to time, may, because of the way they are packaged, the way they are developed, have a different reliability factor.

So I would like to ask what you foresee in the future with regard to the reliability factor of information? Do you anticipate that perhaps in this field, as we become more expert in handling it, the reliability will have, let's say, an improved level? Or is it that you feel that we have started a trend, unfortunately, that would be to-ward lesser reliability?

As I see it, we are involved in an area where the response of the public has been phenomenal. I think it is something in which we all inherently believe, that all feel we are part of. Finding remedies, of course, is the actual and ultimate problem. Because of the great interest at this early stage we are, I am afraid, running around in more than one direction.

My question to you then, Mr. Ross, is, "What is your view of the reliability factor now and for the future?"

Steven S. Ross: I wish I could be optimistic, but my own feeling is that the signal-to-noise ratio continues to worsen year by year, I think, partly because there are more signals. Everybody is getting into the environmental publications business; even publications that had been peripherally interested in it, such as occupational health books, for instance. They tack "Environmental" to their names and immediately start covering environmental subjects.

Perhaps five or ten years ago the private publishers entered the journal publishing business in a big way. Their primary purpose was to make money, which in itself is not evil. You know it is from the desire to make money that we have competition, which results in an improvement in the ultimate product.

However, in publications it just doesn't seem to be working that way. I think all too many publications, perhaps not a majority, but all too many, seem to feel that there are five or six hundred suckers somewhere in the world who can be sold this publication at an inflated price. Not only that, but more people want to fool you now than ever before.

Every morning a number of news releases, most of them announcing things that didn't have to be announced, reach my desk. For example, a company announces the publication of its 1971 edition of its new catalog. So what? This sort of thing ends up cluttering your news pages. Single-man operations can fill publications with absolutely no effort whatsoever.

If I wanted to sit down and publish an eight-page newsletter on this environmental business, I could put one out for about $20,000 a year, $15,000 of which would be my salary, the rest for mailing costs. I could read the New York Times, the Wall Street Journal, the Federal Register; and make sure that every manufacturer in sight who knows my address sends me releases. I don't want to do this. I refuse to do this. Quite a few people aren't so honest.

We have many, many newsletters and other information services from Washington, for instance, that are essentially phony. They are looking for that extra eight or ten thousand dollars a year. They have low-rent offices or boxes in the National Press Building where they clip the UP and the AP, etc. which come into the building free for the use of all the people there. They get the Government press releases. They put something out as a biweekly newsletter or a monthly newsletter, they get publicity for it, and get four or five hundred subscribers tied up in it for a couple of years after which they kill it.

This makes for a bad reputation for the field and makes it difficult for reputable publications to promote themselves. It now costs you on the order of $100 to get a new subscriber through direct mail, because so many people are turned off by newsletters or certain journals. No, I am not optimistic at all.

Moderator Tuwiner: Thank you. Did you want to comment, Mr. Brenner?

Everett H. Brenner (Manager, Central Abstracting and Indexing Service, American Petroleum Institute): I want to get provocative. There is another side.

I gave a talk at SLA two years ago about the mess of the abstracting service publication in this area, and I gave concrete examples of what the Government was doing and what they were producing at that time. For instance, I remember receiving on my desk a governmental publication with abstracts in it; Volume I, No. 1. No date or explanation of the reason for its existence was offered. Some of the material it contained was old and some of it up-to-date.

I kept getting this publication intermittently until I received a copy which said, "Excuse us for being late." I didn't even know when I was supposed to get one, let alone when it was supposed to be late.

That is the condition of the information you are talking about. Thinking to arouse the anger of all these librarians, I said, "Don't you think we ought to do something about this document? I think we ought to organize to stop this kind of thing." I said, "I will do it if you tell me to. If anybody who is interested will just write me a note, I will organize a protest."

I didn't get one note. There were about five hundred people in attendance at this meeting, but I didn't get one letter. We just don't do anything about this. We accept this kind of bad quality.

Moderator Tuwiner: One thing Mr. Ross said puzzled me. He said that there is less reliability, that the signal-to-noise ratio seems to be getting worse. He ascribed this to a great number of signals. I think it might be more logical to ascribe it to a greater amount of noise which seems to be coming mainly from public relations people.

I would now like to present Dr. C.E. Schildknecht.

Dr. C.E. Schildknecht (Consultant): I think there has been little said here about the importance of the human element in all literature searching.

I have written research reports myself out of literature as well as the laboratory, and I have evaluated others. The human element is always going to be important in spite of the computer.

One technique is to get chemical abstracts, and then the addresses of people who produced these latest developments. Write to them. You will be amazed. People like to be recognized. They like to give you their reprints. Write to these people and ask for their reprints and any subsequent material. Very often, amazingly, we get personal letters telling us of developments which haven't yet been published.

In addition, information is often missed because there is no cross-indexing. When you find someone doing experimental work, remember to check for other work by that author. Very often you may find a whole different field.

Moderator Tuwiner: The last member of our panel is Dr. Robert Strickman.

Dr. Robert Strickman: I would like to address my remarks to Mr. Ross, Dr. Schildknecht and Mr. Sittig.

One of the things that has come up here is that there are thousands of bits of information. How do the people who abstract all this information define quality; and how do you define quality in your abstracting service? On a scale going from zero to 100%, would you rate it 10% efficient?

Mr. Ross: Many of the abstracting services, of course, do not find themselves in the position to define what is a quality piece of research, so they merely do an abstract on it, plaster it down, and let the guy that does the search worry about it.

In Air and Water News, where we had very very limited space, I tried to cram everything into eight pages. The few times we went to ten or twelve pages the subscribers complained of the length. You do have to make a value judgment. I make a value judgment as to what is most useful for my particular audience, and here again it comes back to every publication, every person's needs in publications. Both the type of publication and the sophistication of a publication differ. You try to find an editor or publication whose views as to what is most important to the reader matches yours. Admittedly this is a trial and error method and one which makes it very tough on librarians.

Also reputable publications, especially newspapers, weeklies, and bi-weeklies, which have to get information out fast and are in competition with other publications or information services will make errors. God knows I have been fooled often enough by both industry and even enforcement officials on the significance of a piece of data.

Every state enforcement agency will send you a release in a first class, air mail, special delivery letter in which they announce a discovery. For instance, a release from one State last year made the statement that almost all the cars that the State had tested on the road failed to meet the emissions standards that the State had set.

When I got the release, my immediate reaction was to find out what the raw data looked like; how many had failed and by how much did they fail. I called the State and they said that it was just terrible, not anywhere near their expectations. I said, "Send me a report, quick!"

Meanwhile the dailies and some other publications had run with the release, so we also ran with the release, in which I noted that we hadn't seen the whole report. Then I saw the report. Air and Water News comes out on Monday. It went to press on Friday. On that Monday I received the report and looked through the data myself and while it was obvious that almost all the cars had indeed failed to meet the emissions standards they, for the most part, had come extremely close. And, if you made allowance for the accuracy of the test procedure they used, you could see that the conclusions in the release were possibly not justified.

Of course we ate crow and the next week published a correction. Ours was the only one of all the publications that issued the report which had taken the trouble to look at the data.

Nevertheless, even for us it did not end here. People who get newsletters want to bind them in binders, so we publish a quarterly index newsletter which is meant to get information to you. Since this information is not necessarily information that has good staying power, it is published quarterly. In our own index we made this correction and noted that there was a correction from one issue to another. But we were picked up by abstracting services and they didn't catch the correction. When this happens, quite often, you don't catch the error in your literature search.

Using an abstract is fine as a starting point or to return to after you have done your own literature search to ensure that you have missed nothing or to pick up some additional material. It behooves you to remember that abstracting is usually done by housewives, people working part time, students, beginning reporters. I am an old part time abstract writer myself.

But there is nothing that replaces good hard work and I think the honest exhilaration of plowing through information in the library, especially a library with semi-open stacks and a library that has the books on hand, is rewarding. Using a computerized index is no substitute.

Mr. Brenner: I wish I had been here this morning. I wish I had heard you. There are definite guidelines. There are good abstracts. There are guidelines to abstracting. There are abstracting publications that have full time editors. We have a manual. We give a test to the abstracter who comes in. We have professional abstracters. And even though the chemical abstracts have been bad, they have improved over the years.

Engineering Index was a horror at one time. It is better now than ever before. There are criteria for getting up-to-date information. What bothers me are the people who seem to accept them, good or bad. Librarians subscribe to publications and accept information no matter what form it is in.

Mr Ross: My point was that many of the abstracting services and publications that jumped into the environmental field leave much to be desired. God knows, we are depending on abstracting services almost every day. It is a vital part of our life.

Furthermore, strange as it may seem, there are many engineers who have never seen the inside of a library, who wouldn't want to see the inside of a library even if they were dragged in kicking and screaming.

It is not a question of not using an abstracting service or indexing service, but rather a question of relying on it to the exclusion of getting in there and digging on your own. That is the point.

Mr. Sittig: I think I would like to make a comment on this business. I think Dr. Strickman's question was directed not so much to the quality of the abstract preparation but rather how to separate genuine pollution information from the solid waste.

My own personal experience has been to a considerable extent with patent literature. And I think one sure thing is that there is no substitute for interesting someone in the literature information business who has also had the opportunity to work in a plant.

If you have ever worked in chemical manufacturing, I think one good test you can apply to a patent is to read the patent and ask yourself the question: "Would I care to be working the graveyard shift in a plant that was running the process described in the patent?" I think if you answer that question positively you are probably reading a patent that describes a reasonable process.

One other comment I would like to make on the environmental business. We have an instant big business. When you look back in time some ten years, certainly even five years, we are in a great big business in which there were no practitioners very few years ago.

Not many years ago the only people in the environmental business were the sanitary engineers in Civil Engineering. Today you have people in the environment field who are retreaded something elses. They were once aerospace engineers. This is no criticism of the people; it happens to be a situation we were all forced into and one which aggravates the information problem.

Moderator Tuwiner: I just want to say, taking up the matter of patents again, that I have had to spend a considerable amount of time in the Patent Office making searches, and in the public search room I noticed all around me young kids, college kids at the most, maybe even high school age. Every so often a patent attorney would come around and say, "What have you got?" And he gathers up all the data which then turn up in patent searches.

I would like to open the discussion to the audience now.

Dick Berry (Metcalf & Eddy): There is a great Government source which can be used as a basic book for testing other Government information which comes from the Bureau of the Budget. It is a three-volume annual condensation of the U.S. Budget. If you want to read what the Government is doing in the environmental area, read that. In the Budget they tell you what has been spent. The EPA produces figures on what is going to happen, what it is going to do. The Budget tells you what they have done and you can see where the differences lie. It is hard reading, but there are five or six sections of that Budget of four or five pages each which bear very specifically on environment. It is really worth it.

Mr. Brenner: What were your conclusions when you read it?

Mr. Berry: Taking a look at projected items in the grant program for waste treatment facilities, for example, provides a basis for determining the direction that either President Nixon or Mr. Ruckelshaus intends to pursue for the next two to three years.

The Bureau of the Budget presents a record of what has been done on the program, say, in the past five or six years, and it presents the next two-year budget forecast. It is that simple. Not the long-term years, ten year, $7 billion, $12 billion Congressional plans, but the next two years' budget, the budgetary forecast.

If you plot several two-year forecasts along with the actual expenditures you will find that for the last five years the Government grant program on sewage treatment facilities, HUD and EPA together, has risen $50 million a year, year after year over the previous year. It hasn't gone up $400 million this year and $800 million the following. I predict it will go up $50 million more for the next few years and by 1975-1978 it will level off and in the '80s it will decline somewhat.

What I am talking about is interpreting the real information given out. Give yourself a base book. I don't think you can interpret everything you read until you know what has actually happened.

Mr. Sittig: I would like to make one comment on the use of the Federal Budget. There are some interesting numbers in the Budget in the environmental area. I think the point to be emphasized though is that essentially it is a political document. It reflects what the President hopes the Congress will react to.

I think the gross amounts that are stated in that Federal Budget for environmental control are overstated for the purposes of political impressions. For example, you build military barracks in Hawaii and put toilets in them. Somehow their cost may have been subverted in the accounting process to environmental control. You have to be very cautious.

Mr. Berry: Rather than reading the budgetary forecasts, start with real expenditures and do you own trend forecasts. At least you go back to a base book of information.

Moderator Tuwiner: I am glad this symposium is terminating on a note of realism. I am sure whatever was said about Federal budgets can be said equally well, with equal justification, of most State budgets.

We will call this meeting adjourned.

SECTION II

Selected papers presented at the National
Environmental Symposium, sponsored by
the Environmental Protection Agency, held
at Cincinnati, Ohio, September 24-27, 1972.

TECHNICAL INFORMATION PROGRAMS IN THE ENVIRONMENTAL PROTECTION AGENCY

A.C. Trakowski
Deputy Assistant Administrator for Program Operations
Office of Research and Monitoring
Environmental Protection Agency

Today's topic is environmental information and data systems. Somehow it has become fashionable to speak of these two concepts as though they were one and synonymous. Although there is overlap and mutual dependency between data and information, the systems for handling them are not the same, or necessarily even compatible, and they do not necessarily serve the same purposes or users. I've been involved in the design and operation of both types of systems, and I'm conscious of the similarities and differences. Your deliberations should address the problems that both separate and connect environmental data and information systems and their users. But for this moment, let me talk about both, and how we in EPA see them. Let me say a little about what's going on in EPA.

We are all too aware that the products of our activity, our research, our technological development and our surveillance of the environment are data and information. The usefulness and value of these products depend upon their timely availability to the using public. The complexity of the environmental problems facing us today requires the best possible generation, coordination, and dissemination of our data and information, and we are well aware that the management and use of environmental data and information must be improved.

The formation of EPA and the experiences of the past twenty months of operation have reemphasized the interrelatedness of our environmental problems. The many factors of this complexity are directly transposed into the data and information that must be handled and used to serve our national needs. Let me mention a few of these problem factors.

First, the volume alone of environmental data and information is growing at a staggering rate. There are now some 47 different Federal programs producing or serving as outlets for information on air pollution alone.

Second, is the interdisciplinary nature of this information. As we all know, our environmental problems have to be solved as total problems, in which all the pollutants and the total ecology of a domain are considered. We must deal with many technical disciplines such as physics, biology, chemistry, medicine, all branches of engineering and mathematics. We must also consider the fields of psychology, sociology, management, urban planning, economics and law, to name a few. The solution to any environmental problem centers on no one discipline; it involves many. And any solution is usually not unique, but is among several alternatives, each involving a different set of disciplinary components.

A third kind of problem we face with our environmental data and information is that there are a variety of kinds of people who need to use this information. The information must support the scientists and technologists in agencies at the federal, state and municipal levels, in academia and in private industry. Also needing information are the managers and program operatives of these organizations, legislators and concerned citizen and the press, and all sorts of non-technical people who need to act on scientific and technical information.

A fourth problem we have with our environmental data and information is that it can be found almost anywhere. Environmental information is not unique to agencies having missions in environmental matters. Information in other organizations useful to environmental problems must be identified and shared. Without knowledge of what is available in other systems, duplicative and overlapping environmental informations systems tend to spring up. Often the managers of existing centers and proponents of new centers do not know that systems and data banks that can serve their needs exist elsewhere.

We are aware that the forces demanding environmental data and information are very strong. We are also aware of the feelings of frustration in people who cannot seem to gain the material they so sorely need. We are aware that these feelings tend to generate disregard of the systems that exist as unresponsive, and support movement toward a new and omnibus central system that will totally serve all needs. One vision seems to be a cubic mile of computers in Kansas into which all environmental information from anywhere is put, and from which all environmental information to anywhere can be sent instantly, in any combination and for any purpose.

At EPA we observe that in our own agency and throughout the nation, we are already heavily invested in ongoing and rapidly developing information and data systems that contain environmental material. We also see that it is their separation and uncoordinated functioning that frustrates the users. Unless a user knows which system contains what he wants, it is unlikely that he will find it.

Our alternative to a new cubic mile of computers is to extract maximum utility from the systems that we already have, and reserve development of new systems only for functions that cannot be handled by adaptation or extension of existing systems. Our vision then is the development of a system of systems such that material anywhere in the component systems can be retrieved through use of an integrating and interactive network. This network cannot be built in a day. It must evolve as the component information systems, each needed for some specific purpose, are improved, and as the most effective relationships among these systems are found.

The first step is to determine the requirements of that network and the functions of the individual systems of which our network will be composed. We must ask ourselves what information and data we must have to fulfill our many needs.

When setting up the EPA, the President said:

> "Both by itself and together with other agencies,
> the EPA would monitor the conditions of the en-
> vironment — biological as well as physical. With
> these data, the EPA would be able to establish quan-
> titative 'environmental baselines' — critical if we are
> to measure adequately the success or failure of our
> pollution abatement efforts."

Following this guidance, one of our first steps in building our information network at EPA is a study which has three major purposes.

We are also making a survey of EPA computer equipment and facility needs to determine how best to optimize equipment utility and physical location with information system needs. In addition, EPA Information Centers have been identified and steps have been taken to strengthen the links among these facilities.

I could not possibly describe to you the status of all of EPA's current data and information systems within the time I have here today. However, I would like to give you a quick overview of our present capabilities in ten different areas. If you are interested in more detail about these or other capabilities, I understand they will be the subject of informal forum sessions tonight.

First, our Office of Public Affairs. This office provides cohesive public information services and support to Agency programs and operations. It develops public information including publications, audiovisual materials, and exhibits. Special attention is given to schools, youth groups, civic action groups and private citizens.

Second, our EPA Library System. It consists of some 37 libraries. There are libraries at headquarters, in all regional offices except Denver and Atlanta, at each of our four National Environmental Research Centers, and specialized information centers in satellite laboratories and program offices. The collections of any of these libraries are available to the EPA staff at any location.

The National Environmental Research Center here in Cincinnati is the central technical focal point for the Agency library system for cataloging all scientific and technical books for the Agency.

Other libraries in the National Environmental Research Centers, Regional Offices, and laboratories serve as liaison for the system with university, state and local government, private organizations, environmental libraries and publishing offices in their locations, in order to provide EPA with the broadest possible coverage of all environmental information.

Our computer generated Journal Holdings Report includes all journals received by any library in the system, and the computer generated Book Holdings file will permit immediate cataloging of any items already in the system. Bibliographies resulting from computer literature searches or manual methods will be available through normal distribution channels and the Department of Commerce's National Technical Information Service.

(1) identifying national requirements for environ-
     mental pollution data;
(2) comparing these requirements with data collec-
     tion activities and resources already available
     within EPA and other Federal agencies; and
(3) identifying those requirements for environmental
     pollution data which are not being satisfied
     and which should have higher priority for the
     commitment of new resources.

Once this study is completed, we will be in a position to design
whatever systems are needed to coordinate and improve the utilization of environmental data. We will look at the feasibility of integrating monitoring subsystems among the various media.

Under the reorganization plan which created EPA, the environmental programs of several agencies were consolidated into EPA. Resulting from this consolidation were the inherited problems of com-
partmentalization, fragmentation and duplication. We have had to
harmonize these different elements, among them the area of information resources. Over 50 separate information facilities — libraries
and information centers — were passed on to EPA. Supporting these
information facilities was a wide range of data handling equipment,
and computer hardware and software packages.

To resolve this confusion, our agency in 1971 formed an Information
Systems Committee. The group is composed of personnel from EPA
Headquarters, EPA's ten regional offices, and EPA's laboratories
throughout the country. Its objectives are: (1) to identify gaps in
meeting the information needs of EPA managers and program oper-
ators; (2) to identify possible overlaps and duplications in the existing systems and data bases; (3) to identify systems training and
orientation needs at all levels of EPA management and operations;
(4) to develop standard data elements and codes for common-use
items of information; and (5) to recommend Agency-wide information management policies and programs.

We are at work conducting a comprehensive inventory of EPA information systems. The results will be used for research, analytic
and reference purposes. It will include the production of a dictionary of systems, construction of a profile of the kind of information
currently available and proposed to be available, and determination
of how current systems may be used analytically as interactive tools
for research in addition to the library mode of use.

Third, our information systems in the area of air pollution control. EPA, since 1967, has accumulated over 20 million air quality (Storage and Retrieval of Aerometric Data) data values and 6 million sources inventory and emissions data values. The data bases (National Emission Data System) are expanding at the rate of several millions of values per year. These values come from internal EPA sources, state, local and other Federal agencies, the World Health Organization, the World Meteorological Organization and from non-government groups. Currently, the system is accessible only by EPA's National Air Data Branch, but remote terminal access from the EPA Regional Offices is being initiated.

Our Air Pollution Technical Information Center (APTIC), in North Carolina, now has records on over 43,000 documents, with an increase of 700 to 1,000 per month. The sources of the documents referenced by the system include EPA air pollution manuscripts, government reports, more than 1,100 domestic and foreign serial publications, patents, technical society papers, dissertations, translations, and articles from books and proceedings. With this record base, APTIC conducts literature searches which result in abstracts from the complete file and from the latest month's additions, to produce Air Pollution Abstracts, a monthly publication sold by the Government Printing Office (GPO), and to produce bibliographies and state-of-the-art summaries for printing and sale by GPO.

In the future, APTIC hopes to provide access to EPA's regional offices and to state and local air pollution control agencies by remote terminals.

The fourth information system I would like to discuss is in the area of water pollution. STORET, a system initiated in 1963, is the central computer-oriented segment of EPA's National Water Quality Surveillance and Information System for storing and retrieving data and information on water quality; water quality standards; pollution-caused fish kills; manpower and training needs; municipal and industrial waste discharges; and waste abatement needs, costs and implementation schedules.

There are presently 42 Federal terminals throughout the country for on-line access to STORET. Twenty states also have terminals. EPA is encouraging the use of this system by other Federal, state and local agencies. Adding users to the STORET system will reduce duplication of information gathering efforts, and gain the use of data and information gathered by those agencies at much lower cost than would be possible otherwise. The material in STORET is necessary to EPA management decisions such as definition of pollution problem areas, prioritied allocation of Agency efforts toward abatement and control, determination of trends in water quality control programs, identification of specific polluting wastewater courses, and municipal waste treatment facility construction needs.

The system also supports technical and scientific studies. For example, a large field study may result in thousands of data values. STORET can perform the function of a filing and classifying system and a data statistical analysis and evaluation system.

In addition to STORET, dissemination of water quality information is provided by the Water Resources Scientific Information Center (WRSIC) of the Department of the Interior under a cooperative arrangement. EPA supports eight "centers of competence," largely at universities, which produce indexed abstracts in their respective fields. These are then published by WRSIC as part of Selected Water Resources Abstracts.

The fifth information capability I want to mention is in the area of pesticides. We are publishing two key periodicals here. One is the Health Aspects of Pesticides Abstract Bulletin. The other is the Pesticides Monitoring Journal, an interdepartmental publication.

A combined effort of the Toxicology Information Program of the National Library of Medicine, the Food and Drug Administration and EPA's Division of Pesticide Community Studies, which publishes the abstract I just mentioned, has produced a generalized on-line storage and retrieval system, TOXICON. It accepts abstracts and data coming from the various contributing programs in a standardized format. I understand that TOXICON is now available to the public, with access to the system by remote terminals.

Sixth, in the area of solid waste management, EPA offers the only known specialized literature coverage of the solid waste field. Our Solid Waste Information Retrieval System (SWIRS) covers the published information concerning current research and technological developments in the solid waste management field worldwide. Computerization of the record base of approximately 18,000 references has been completed. SWIRS also provides a bulletin of condensed abstracts of current acquisitions, which is published bimonthly.

Seventh is the EPA Office of Research and Monitoring's information system. We have established a new service called ENVIRON, which stands for Environmental Information Retrieval On-Line. ENVIRON is an on-line, interactive information retrieval system.

ENVIRON is oriented towards information retrieval problems which are characterized by difficult and vague subject definition, extensive variance in term selection, changing scientific and technical terminology, and imprecise search definition. Other government agencies, such as The National Library of Medicine and NASA, have adopted the same computer software included in ENVIRON. The use of this common software could obviously improve the intergovernmental exchange of environmental information in several ways.

As I said before, ENVIRON is a new system. So far, six files have been installed in the system.

(1) EPA Ongoing Research Projects. This system will describe all currently active EPA research and development projects, whether in-house or by contract, grant or interagency agreement arrangement.

(2) Technical Assistance Data. This is a file of data on oil and hazardous materials to provide quick access to technical information on the hazardous compounds for technical assistance to pollution problems.

(3) Oil and Hazardous Materials Incidence. This file covers information on oil and hazardous materials pollution events, including details of their locations and recovery activities.

(4) Water Quality Surveillance Network directory of all STORET sampling stations, where they are and what they measure.

(5) Industrial Waste Abstracts, a file of selected articles and abstracts from industrial waste publications.

(6) EPA final research reports, a file of reports produced from EPA research and development project efforts.

The eighth information capability I want to talk about is in a new part of our Office of Research and Monitoring. Technology Transfer, as this function is called, is concerned with active transfer of the methods and techniques resulting from EPA's research and development to practical use by the public.

Our Technology Transfer program has several vehicles for getting information to users. Most important, it has so far developed four process design manuals for design engineers which describe the state-of-the-art in water pollution control technology. These loose-leaf manuals wrap up EPA in-house, contract and grant research; other Federal research; other governmental research and private industry research into a format and content suitable for use by municipal, state and private consulting engineers.

The current design manuals have been distributed widely through the engineering community. The Technology Transfer program is now expanding into all areas of pollution control. First among these new areas will be air pollution and solid waste. Also, to communicate new technologies to state and local government decision makers, Technology Transfer has prepared a number of semi- or non-technical publications.

The ninth information system of EPA which should be mentioned is our new technical information system for noise. The Noise Information Service (NOISE) will contain initially citations and abstracts of various publications. These records are directly accessible from a remote computer terminal. In the future, files on such areas as noise research and noise programs may be created. This system uses the same software package used by ENVIRON, the record base will soon become a part of ENVIRON, and it will be accessible to the public through EPA's Office of Noise Abatement and Control or through its Regional Offices.

And now, the tenth and last area of information capability which I would like to mention. The National Environmental Policy Act of 1969 (NEPA) requires all Federal agencies to assess the environmental impact of their programs and the activities that they support, and file an Environmental Impact Statement. EPA is one of the major commenting agencies on these statements. To manage its Environmental Impact Statement review process, EPA maintains in a central computer system a continuing record of the content and action on statements being reviewed. Inquiries can be made on federal projects that are expected to effect the environment and on what those effects may be (Office of Federal Activities).

We have a long road ahead of us in improving and integrating these capabilities, but I think we have made very substantial progress. Of course, our system integration will also include attachments to information systems outside of EPA.

In closing, I would like to point out that this symposium is of great importance to us in EPA. The scheduling of EPA efforts for development of a network of environmental information systems has been arranged so that we might take advantage of the results of this symposium as part of our decision-making processes. EPA must consider carefully the views of the users of environmental information before making long-term commitments. These commitments will include establishing integrated information facilities, purchasing computer and telecommunications equipment to process and transmit data and information, and establishing methods to insure that stored documents and items of data are properly correlated, indexed, easily retrievable and effectively presented.

We hope you will use this symposium to let us know what you think and what you need. We believe our data and information systems must serve not only our Agency, but must also serve you.

THE EDS ENVIRONMENTAL
SCIENCE INFORMATION CENTER

James E. Caskey
Director, ESIC

The Environmental Science Information Center (ESIC) is the new name of NOAA's former Scientific Information and Documentation Division, which was transferred to the Environmental Data Service (EDS) on July 11, 1971. Under EDS, ESIC will retain responsibility for all of NOAA's scientific and technical publication, information and library activities. This literature-based information center will complement the EDS family of data centers, enhancing the service structure EDS needs to provide a comprehensive, one-stop source for data and information applicable to environmental problems.

As NOAA's publisher, ESIC guides the flow of scientific and technical manuscripts from NOAA's research laboratories and technical service offices through appropriate channels of scientific reviewing, editorial processing and printing, then monitors the dissemination of NOAA's publications to scientific, technical, engineering, agricultural, industrial and governmental users. The objectives of these editing and publishing services, provided by ESIC's Scientific and Technical Publication Division, are:

(1) to apply scientific and editorial quality standards to NOAA's technical manuscripts to enhance their scientific value; and

(2) to provide suitable media for prompt publication and wide dissemination of the results of NOAA's research, technological development and technical services.

As NOAA's "information banker," ESIC serves as a national focus for literature-based information in the marine, atmospheric and earth sciences and their related technologies. Its Technical Information Divison collects, indexes, abstracts and announces scientific and technical publications relevant to NOAA's missions and fields of service. Storing, retrieving and extracting information from its own bibliographic and research project data banks and those of other organizations, the Division is developing a single-stop environmental science information service for NOAA's users.

As NOAA's librarian, ESIC coordinates NOAA's library services. The Libraries Division operates two major environmental science libraries (the Atmospheric Sciences Library in Silver Spring, Md. and the Marine and Earth Sciences Library in Rockville, Md.), a Technical Processes Branch, and a Field Libraries Branch, and functionally supervises about 30 NOAA field libraries scattered throughout the country. Two interrelated ESIC long-range objectives are:

(1)   to link these libraries into a coordinated NOAA library system; and

(2)   to tie the system into the NOAA information network, so that the library collections may be tapped readily by all users who could benefit from these valuable sources of environmental science information.

By transferring these functions from a staff office to the Environmental Data Service, a line component, and integrating its scientific and technical editing, publishing, information and library activities into the EDS network of environmental data centers, NOAA has linked ESIC to additional communications channels capable of amplifying its services to the total scientific and technical community, to users both inside and outside NOAA.

In EDS, ESIC can place new emphasis on meeting national and international needs for environmental science information, which is as much a national and international resource as environmental data. Both information and data are the cumulative products of science and are essential for the work of future scientists. Gathered from many common sources, processed in similar ways, and often applied to the same problems, environmental information and data resources lend themselves logically to common cultivation and management by EDS.

The characteristics of the problem of cultivating NOAA's environmental science information resources and making them readily available for application are comparable to those brought into sharp focus in the quotation below from a recent UNESCO report (United Nations Educational, Scientific and Cultural Organization and the International Council of Scientific Unions, UNISIST, Synopsis of the Feasibility Study on a World Science Information System, UNESCO, Paris, 1971, 92 pp.) on the international problems of science information:

> "The problem...is a complex one...unfortunately termed the 'information explosion'... Faulty distribution practices and understocked and understaffed libraries make access to these (scientific and technical articles and reports) difficult... These are the familiar characteristics of the problem. Less obvious...are the changing needs of the world scientific community for information. The interdisciplinary approach to problems of the environment, for example, requires information drawn from a variety of sciences: chemistry, biology, sociology, to name only a few.
>
> The emerging needs of applied science, technology and engineering add further complexities. The classic information services, the scientific journals, abstracting and indexing services, [and] libraries, have all demonstrated a cultural lag in accommodating rapidly to these new requirements. The achievement of new and flexible forms of information services, to meet these new needs, is the fundamental problem..."

The establishment of ESIC in EDS opens the way to solving this fundamental problem in the multidiscipline field relevant to NOAA's mission. ESIC will attempt to satisfy new types of demands in the field of environmental science by applying modern computer and communication technologies to its classic information services, and integrating them into the new total system concept of EDS as a single source service for users of environmental data *and* information. This is the role of ESIC in EDS.

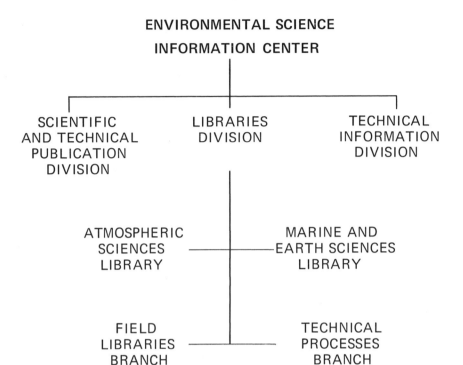

FEDERAL ENVIRONMENTAL
DATA CENTERS AND SYSTEMS

Arnold R. Hull
Associate Director for Climatology
Environmental Data Service, NOAA
U.S. Department of Commerce

INTRODUCTION

Our environment extends from the center of the Earth to the center of the sun. There is hardly any area of human activity in which environmental data are not needed daily to improve man's understanding and use of his environment and its living and nonliving resources.

Every minute of every day, thousands of observations are made concerning the myriad aspects of our environment. Eventually, many of these data, whether collected in the ocean's depths, outer space or a country field, wind up in one of the Federal Government's environmental data centers or systems, where they are generally available to all. The questions I shall answer during this presentation are:

(1) Who has what data?
(2) What specific products and services are available
    to users?
(3) How do users plug into the system?

U.S. DEPARTMENT OF COMMERCE — NATIONAL OCEANIC AND ATMOSPHERIC ADMINISTRATION (NOAA)

NOAA's Environmental Data Service (EDS) operates three environmental data centers: the National Climatic Center (NCC), the

National Oceonographic Data Center (NODC), and the National Geophysical and Solar-Terrestrial Data Center (NGSDC). EDS is also
developing a Great Lakes data center, temporarily located within
the NODC. (Another component, the Environmental Science Information Center, provides literature-related system complementary to
EDS' data system.) All centers serve the general public, other Federal agencies, business and industry, the academic community, state
and local governments, and foreign users.

The National Climatic Center

The National Climatic Center (NCC) in Asheville, N.C. is the largest
climatological data center in the world, a unique central source of
historical weather data and related data products. As the collection
center and custodian of all United States weather records, NCC ob-
tains data generated by NOAA's National Weather Service, the
weather services of the Air Force, Navy and Coast Guard, the Federal Aviation Administration, and thousands of cooperative observers.

NCC Data Services and Products: Climatological data available from
NCC include hourly surface meteorological observations from land
stations; 3-hourly and 6-hourly surface observations from land stations, ocean weather stations and moving ships; upper air observations; radar observations; meteorological satellite data; selected maps
and charts originally prepared by NOAA's National Meteorological
Center; derived and summary data and tabulations; special collections such as Barbados Oceonographic-Meteorological Experiment
meteorological data, Global Atmospheric Research Program basic
data set, solar radiation data, and many others.

After computer and human editing, data for which there is general
user demand are summarized and disseminated in a wide variety of
publications. Each year, one million copies of monthly and annual
NCC climatological publications are mailed to 65,000 subscribers.

Other data forms and products available to users include special
summaries, copies of original records or groups of records, magnetic
tapes, computer output to microfilm analyses or graphics, and hand-
prepared tabulations and analyses.

The National Oceanographic Data Center

The National Oceanographic Data Center (NODC) houses the
world's largest accessible collection of marine data. It is the

national repository for historical oceanographic data and data products.

NODC receives data for all oceans, seas and estuaries from hundreds of sources, domestic and foreign, including the national data centers of other countries. Data and publications are also obtained by exchange between the Center and individuals and organizations in 45 countries and such groups as the ICES, the International Council for the Exploration of the Sea, as gifts from scientists and organizations wishing to share their data, and through the purchase of valuable marine data collections.

NODC Data Services and Products: Oceanographic data available from NODC include mechanical and expendable bathy-thermograph data in analog and digital form; oceanographic station data for surface and serial depths; continuously recorded salinity-temperature-depth data in digital form; surface current information; biological data; geological sampling inventory, primarily for the New England Continental Shelf; and bottom sample information.

NODC services and products include: data processing; data reproduction — in computer printout, punch card, magnetic tape, and other forms; analysis and preparation of statistical summaries; evaluation of various data records for specific analytical requirements; library search; referral; provision of general marine sciences information; and publications, including data processing manuals, catalogs of holdings, data reports and atlases.

"The User's Guide for NODC's Data Processing Systems," available from NODC on request, provides detailed information concerning data holdings.

Great Lakes Data Services

In February, 1972, EDS established within NODC a special unit to meet the needs of multidiscipline data users in the Great Lakes drainage area. The unit has proposed a project inventory for the International Field Year for the Great Lakes (IFYGL). The inventory contains about 3,000 computerized records of the data collected this year from Lake Ontario. Although designed primarily for use by United States and Canadian managers for IFYGL, the listing is available to any user interested in environmental data for the Great Lakes area.

National Geophysical and Solar-Terrestrial Data Center

The National Geophysical and Solar-Terrestrial Data Center (NGSDC) is responsible for environmental data in the fields of seismology, geomagnetism, marine geology and geophysics, solar activity, interplanetary phenomena, the ionosphere, cosmic rays, aurorae and airglow.

Seismology: Some 300,000 seismic recordings or seismograms per year from about 150 earthquake-monitoring stations around the globe are processed and archived by the NGSDC's Solid Earth Sciences Division, adding to a file that numbers more than two million seismograms. Accelerograms and data analyses from NOAA's strong-motion seismology program are also part of the Center's seismic holdings.

Geomagnetism: Geomagnetic data are received from United States and foreign sources and consist primarily of worldwide geomagnetic survey measurements and observatory magnetograms, which show changes in direction and strength of the earth's magnetic field, hourly values, and indices of magnetic activity. Holdings include some one million magnetograms, which accumulate at a rate of about 50,000 per year (most are stored on 35 millimeter microfilm). The Solid Earth Data Services Division also compiles United States and World Magnetic Charts, the latter in collaboration with the U.S. Naval Oceanographic Office.

Marine Geology and Geophysics: NGSDC handles gravimetric, magnetic, bathymetric and seismic observations collected at sea by Federal agencies and many universities and research centers, as well as some foreign sources. In addition, NOAA's Environmental Data Service is managing and disseminating marine geophysical data obtained from explorations under the International Decade of Ocean Exploration (IDOE).

Solar Terrestrial Physics: Most of the data managed by the Center's Solar-Terrestrial Data Service Division come from worldwide sources under international exchange agreements. The rapidly expanding file contains more than 11 million feet of ionogram film, 80,000 feet of all-sky camera film, 2.5 million sheets of graphical and numerical data, and additional information on magnetic tape from NOAA and NOAA-supplied stations and several hundred cooperating institutions.

Ionosphere data received include vertical soundings, topside soundings, electron density profiles, systematic observations of ionospheric absorption and drifts, atmospheric radio noise measurements, whistlers, very low frequency noise observations, and other categories. Solar activity data include those on solar flares, radio emission events, sudden ionospheric disturbances, and some satellite monitoring measurements of ultraviolet, x-ray and particle emissions, and the solar wind.

Also included are global solar patrol data on calcium plages, solar magnetic fields and chromospheric structure, various daily maps of the sun, and solar indices. Auroral data consist mainly of all-sky photographs. Cosmic ray observations are made by the world network of ground-based stations.

NGSDC data are available in numerous reports and publications; in microform; on punched cards or magnetic tape; in summaries and tables; and maps, charts and graphs. Marine geological records include cores, samples and best flow and sediment data.

Environmental Data Service User Requests

EDS data and data products are available to users upon request on an exchange basis, at the cost of retrieval and reproduction, or, for publications and certain simple services, at unit costs established by the Department of Commerce. User requests to any of EDS data centers should define the data required, stations or geographical areas of concern, desired format, and a description of the problem for which the data are required.

User-visitors are welcome at the NCC, NODC and NGSDC. Working space and technical assistance are available upon request; advance notice is requested, however, for scheduling purposes.

OTHER CENTERS AND SYSTEMS

In addition to the large-volume centers and systems I have just described, there are other environmental data activities which should be noted. In general, their holdings consist of biological, chemical, geological, or tides and currents data. Brief summaries of specific centers and systems are contained in the "SEQUIP Directory," which should soon be available to the public, either through the Government Printing Office or the Department of Commerce's National Technical Information Service.

WORLD DATA CENTER A — MECHANISM FOR INTERNATIONAL EXCHANGE

The World Data Center A (WDC-A) system was established in the United States as a result of the International Geophysical Year (IGY). Under an agreement with the National Academy of Sciences, NOAA is responsible for WDC-A activities in solar and interplanetary phenomena; ionospheric phenomena; aurorae, cosmic rays and airglow; geomagnetism; gravity; seismology; the Upper Mantle Project Archives; tsunami; and meteorology and nuclear radiation. Glaciology is the responsibility of the U.S. Geological Survey; longitude and latitude of the U.S. Navy, and rockets and satellites of NASA's National Space Science Data Center.

Most of the WDC-A subcenters are identical with or collocated at national centers for the same disciplines. Each regularly exchanges data with WDC-B (Moscow) and WDC-C (countries in Western Europe). In addition, they also receive data from cooperative international programs and, in some cases, from national programs.

The WDC-A system is a nongovernmental program. It was organized under the International Council of Scientific Unions (ICSU), whose constituent bodies are the academies of science of the countries involved — not government agencies. The centers are freely accessible to visiting scientists of any country and, on request, provide copies of their data at cost.

The overall guidance of the World Data Centers is the responsibility of the ICSU panel composed of representatives from each of the major geophysical areas and from the WDC's themselves. The role of the ICSU Panel is to coordinate policies common to all disciplines and to give final approval to guides prepared for the various disciplines by appropriate scientific bodies. The Panel intends to issue in 1972 a consolidated guide that will incorporate guidelines for all scientific areas of concern.

REFERRAL SERVICES — ENDEX

The Stockholm conference has recognized the need for international referral services, as well as the national and local needs. As an example, we might consider the many cooperative coastal zone studies now being contemplated; the various Federal, state, local and private organizations involved cannot intelligently plan their projects without pertinent available data and information; and they certainly do not want to duplicate existing data files through their own collection efforts.

To meet such national needs, NOAA's Environmental Data Service (EDS) is developing ENDEX, an Environmental Data Index. When ENDEX is fully developed, a user will be able to obtain rapid referral to national and international data archives and sources simply by calling an information specialist at any EDS center to "plug into" the interdisciplinary ENDEX system.

EDS is currently documenting collections scattered nationally and internationally, obtaining available inventory and reference materials, and integrating these into the ENDEX system. We are beginning with collections easily accessible and particularly pertinent to contemporary environmental problems.

A LOOK AHEAD

As you can see, there are many disciplines, collectors, processors, and users in the environmental data field. Essentially, the data centers and systems I have discussed exist to serve the user community. To minimize duplication of efforts and get the most out of our data dollar, we must communicate, cooperate and coordinate our efforts. This is the prime reason for this Symposium.

Overall the present trend toward increasing interdisciplinary, interagency and international cooperation and coordination can only accelerate. The "environment" is not divisible; you cannot isolate any one area, whether by discipline, geography or organization, and deal with it realistically. The word "interface" has long since become a cliche with respect to environmental data.

Finally, I would like to repeat Dr. Townsend's invitation for each of you to participate as fully as possible in the Symposium. In our varying roles, each of us is working toward the same goal: an environmental data system capable of efficiently and economically meeting the growing challenges of our common environment.

SCIENTIFIC AND TECHNICAL INFORMATION CENTERS
CONCERNED WITH THE BIOLOGICAL SCIENCES

William B. Cottrell
Director, Nuclear Safety Information Center
Oak Ridge National Laboratory

INTRODUCTION

Thank you Mr. Chairman: Ladies and Gentlemen, it is a pleasure for me to be here today to talk about one of my favorite vocations, scientific information centers. I also feel honored to be sharing this lecture period with my two distinguished colleagues, but after the talks you've already heard on this subject both here and elsewhere, it makes me feel like Zsa Zsa Gabor's fifth husband on their honeymoon; I know what I'm supposed to do, but I don't know if I can make it interesting.

Now whether or not I can indeed make it interesting remains to be seen — but I am certain that you are in this room because you want to learn something about scientific and technical information centers; that you didn't just come in here and sit down because you want to give your feet a rest; that you should be interested in these proceedings. And that comment is by no means limited to what I've got to say; it applies equally well to the other speakers on this afternoon's program and I hope also to the other groups which follow.

At this point I would like to introduce a definition of information centers so that we can all be tuned in on the same wave length. I realize that there is some risk in doing this, as I'll appear much less profound by being clear, simple and straightforward, but *c'est la vie*. I have selected as my starting definition the one developed by the President's Science Advisory Committee in their report "Science Information and Government,"[1] published a decade ago, to wit:

"The specialized information center [is] primarily a technical institute rather than a technical library. It must be led by professional working scientists who maintain the closest contact with their technical professions and who by being near the data can make new syntheses that are denied all those who do not have the [information] at their fingertips. The specialized center should become the accepted retailer of information, switching, interpreting and otherwise processing information from the large wholesale depositories and archival journals to the individual user."

The significant points in this definition are that (1) the center is led by scientists, and (2) they — the scientists — process the information, not just the documents which contain information. At this point, I would like to direct your attention to these significant differences between an information center and a good library.

A library, as well as an information center, may acquire, store, retrieve and disseminate information in the broad sense, but only the information center is prepared to offer technical evaluation of the information thus "processed." Furthermore, the basic unit thus processed by a library is generally a book, journal or document; whereas in the information center it would be the knowledge itself, not necessarily the source in which this knowledge is contained.

This fact brings us to two other significant characteristics of an information center not explicitly included in the preceding definitions: (1) the knowledge which is processed in an information center is "indexed" for retrieval purposes to a much greater depth than in a library, and (2) as a consequence of this processing depth, it is not generally considered practical for information centers to approach the breadth of technical libraries, and in actual practice they have extremely narrow fields of interest.

Up to this point we have talked about information centers and data centers almost interchangeably. As far as this paper is concerned, "information center" is the general term, and a "data center" is merely a unique type of information center in which the knowledge being processed is in numerical form.

With this background I would propose the following definition for scientific information centers: "A scientific information center is an organization, staffed mainly by scientists and engineers, who first index and then compile, analyze, evaluate, condense, extrapolate, and/or synthesize information in a given area as integral steps in a comprehensive information acquisition, storage, retrieval and dissemination process for the benefit of the scientific community to which they belong."

So much for definitions. It is the purpose of my talk to discuss with you the information and the problems and opportunities available from one class of information centers in the U.S.

CENTERS AND ORGANIZATIONS COVERED

My subject area for today's talk is information centers concerned with the biological sciences. In order to further delineate the bounds of each speaker's responsibility this afternoon, we partitioned the centers listed in the directory contained in the SEQUIP report.[2] For those of you who may not know, SEQUIP stands for "Study of Environmental Quality Information Programs" in the Federal Government.

The study was undertaken at a workshop in the spring of 1970. The first draft of the SEQUIP report was distributed in the spring of 1971 and a second draft in 1972. (I hope that doesn't mean that the third draft will be distributed in 1973.) In any event, the SEQUIP Directory lists a total of 73 environmental information and data programs. Of these, 29 dealt primarily in the biological sciences.

A STUDY OF INFORMATION PROVIDED AND TO WHOM

Now I could have rehashed the information in the SEQUIP report on "my" 29 centers for you, and I will to some extent. However, in order to develop additional information besides that in the SEQUIP report, I prepared a questionnaire and sent it to 23 of the 29 centers of interest here as well as to 139 other centers of potential interest. A copy of the questionnaire and cover letter text are included herewith as Appendix A.

I will not report on the results of the larger survey other than to say that only 48% (i.e., 78 out of 162) responded. The response from the SEQUIP centers was considerably better than 65% (i.e., 15 out of 23 inquiries sent), but still much less than one would expect from true information centers organized to serve the technical community. The results of this survey of the 29 SEQUIP centers are summarized in Table 1.

It is not possible at this point in time, or from my position, to say why the other eight centers contacted did not respond. There are at least two obvious reasons: (1) they are not true information centers, and/or (2) they are established to serve a specific mission rather than the technical community in general, or at least, in particular, the technical community represented by my inquiry — which in this case was as a member of the Oak Ridge National Laboratory.

However, analysis of the 15 centers which did respond does provide us with some valuable information on these centers as individual entities, as well as providing us with some interesting insights into the information center business as a whole. The principal points of interest are:

(1)   Who is served?
(2)   What type of information is provided?
(3)   From what information resource?

The survey results on each of these three points are summarized in Tables 2, 3 and 4.

It is not really surprising to see that individuals, without connections, are the least served, i.e., 61%. Perhaps, on the other hand, it is surprising that such a large fraction of the centers will apply their technical resources to the needs of an individual per se. The only other surprise in the matter of users is that while 85% of the centers will serve government contractors, only 70% will serve other government agencies.

There was almost complete unanimity in center function and in the preparation of reports. All centers did so (except the Patent Office which has a distinctly different function anyway). This proclivity toward report preparation would be expected from the very nature and purpose of technical information centers, even if not because, as government entities, one would expect such a product anyway. In addition to report preparation all centers, with two exceptions, answer technical inquiries and provide technical consultation — other functions which are commonly expected of technical information centers.

Most centers (77%) also prepare bibliographies (both general and specific) and presumably provide this bibliographic information as needed in response to specific request. In fact, several centers have their information files computerized so that bibliographic searches may be programmed to the specific needs of the user. Not surprisingly, only 30% of the centers provide SDI — one of these charges for this service and others are considering doing so. Only 30% of the centers have a newsletter as such, although several others have periodic publications which serve this purpose to some extent.

Considering the limited statistics, it is a little more difficult to come up with significant numbers in terms of documents processed per center technical staff member, since this number is influenced so greatly by the other functions of the center. Thus, while the ranges indicated are taken directly from the survey returns, the mean values might better be defined as best judgment values where one-third to one-half of the technical staff time is spent in assessing information and the remainder in the preparation of reports and other services.

In this discussion of response to this survey, it is also noteworthy that only 5 of the 15 centers which responded enclosed the brochure that was requested. This would suggest that there is room for improvement in the mechanics of our operations to avoid such simple oversights.

RESULTS OF A SPECIFIC INFORMATION REQUEST

It is one thing for a center to identify the services it provides and to whom in response to a survey; it could be an entirely different thing to obtain information under "field" conditions. Therefore, being inherently an experimentalist and possibly also somewhat of a skeptic, I thought I'd conduct a little experiment. Accordingly, I wrote to each of the centers and presented each with a practical information inquiry within the scope of their center.

In order to maintain the objectivity of this experiment, I assumed the identity of a corporate research director doing graduate work on an environmental problem under a corporation scholarship. With the information provided by the centers, I was then in a position to evaluate their response.

A typical inquiry is included herewith as Appendix B and consists of a letter giving my assumed background and interest in a particular area following which it identified two or three specific topics and requested three items: (1) a bibliography on the specific topic; (2) an opinion on a specific issue; (3) a brochure of the center. I also requested the response within two weeks.

The results are summarized in Table 5. The number of centers listed there is 27 since I omitted my center, NSIC, and No. 68 since the reply stated their work is handled by center No. 26.

Of the 27 information programs contacted, four or 15% did not respond at all. Of the 23 which responded the average response time was 11 days, with 17 of the centers getting their reply back within the two-week period as requested. Two of the centers, i.e., No. 62, Science Information Exchange and No. 31, Environmental Systems Applications Centers, expressed a willingness to provide information, but had a charge for doing so. I did not proceed further in the evaluation of these centers.

My evaluation was based upon the relevance of the response to the questions asked, the usefulness of the material which was provided (bibliographies and/or documents), and the assistance provided by the technical consultant in the responding cover letter including especially the opinion which was requested. I am sure that any other evaluation would come up with a different rating, since the matter is so subjective; also one sample from a center is no adequate indication of its overall effectiveness. Hence, I would ask that this evaluation be kept in perspective for whatever merits it may have in assessing averages and for the insight it provides to the problem of information communication and not to stigmatize any center.

Nevertheless, from the point of view of a prospective user, the response from these inquiries was extremely gratifying in some instances and very disappointing in others. I have rated half (14) of the responses as Satisfactory (A or B). The other half (13) included four which did not reply at all, two that charged for such services, one which wanted more information, and the remaining seven from whom the replies were just inadequate. In addition to the bibliographies which I requested, I have received enough documents to start a small library. This came about from two principal factors: first, several centers, which apparently were not equipped to provide special bibliographic searches, sent large published bibliographies and/or copies of abstract publications; and second, many centers volunteered copies of relevant articles on the subject in question.

Only about half of the replies addressed themselves to the specific issue regarding which I had asked their opinion, but in only a few instances did I have the impression that a qualified technical person had provided me with any real insights on the problem. I fared a little better this time in obtaining brochures, since eleven of the centers contacted sent same, as opposed to the five brochures which were returned in response to the general survey.

Another interesting bit of information relates to the return communiques themselves. Half (14) of the centers responded using official government envelopes for which no postage was required; of these all were first class except three which responded by airmail. Of the remainder, most were nongovernment organizations operating under contract to a government agency, but under such an arrangement they have to pay postage. These responses included two third class mailings and one airmail, the remainder being first class.

DISCUSSION

A person with an information need first must find out where he can go to have his need serviced. This in itself is more difficult than it would appear as it involves the answers to several related questions, e.g.:

(1)   What information centers have a technical scope which includes my need?
(2)   Do each of these relevant centers provide the service I desire?
(3)   Am I eligible to receive services from all of these centers?
(4)   Is there any charge for these services?
(5)   What size technical staff do they have?
(6)   How long will it take to get the desired information?

Some, but not all of the above, is provided by the various compilations of information centers which exist.[2][3][4][5]   On the other hand, I have attempted here to provide the remaining information for the SEQUIP centers in this article.

Of course, one of the biggest problems in soliciting information is that the name of a group is often misleading as to its technical scope. Another problem lies in the fact that many groups and organizations that are popping up these days on lists of information programs are not prepared to provide information to the "outside" user and probably should not have been listed in the first place. If you have any doubt about the responsibility of any group, it would be better to talk to them first and find out what they are indeed constituted to do. Again, the information in this paper will give you some insight as to what to expect from the SEQUIP centers.

The concept of talking with a center (or visiting same in person) before initiating an inquiry will in most cases save you time, the center time, and result in the most satisfactory response. By so doing this, the user's needs can be best matched to the center's information scope and services, thereby achieving a better result than is normally possible from a simple letter request. Talking with the center also helps direct attention to your important problem and overcomes such obstacles as the center's apparent inability to read (witness the previously cited difficulty in getting brochures). Such personal contact is also more likely to result in your request receiving the attention you would like, both as far as the timeliness of the response is concerned, as well as focusing the attention of the technical expert on your problem — where an opinion is desired.

Several centers are automated so that the incremental cost of providing a user with certain information is minimal. These special bibliographies can be prepared in minutes (although a day is more reasonable) and SDI are routinely sent to thousands of users. In fact, the capabilities of centers are so enhanced by such automation that I would expect it to become an essential requirement in the very near future for all but some of the smallest, most specialized centers.

Most centers neither provide nor sell the documents they may refer you to. Hence, one should anticipate that the response from an information center will not completely solve your problem, but provide you with the awareness of the existing tools for the job. The rest is up to the user.

CONCLUSIONS

(1) Not all information programs listed in the SEQUIP report and other compilations are technical information centers constituted to provide information outside the sponsoring agency.

(2) For true technical information centers there are significant differences, as well as similarities in the users served and the services provided which should be confirmed in some manner before initiating a request.

(3) Information responses vary widely and are most relevant and meaningful when the user understands what he can expect, and the center understands the user's needs. This is best achieved by some personal contact (as by phone) in addition to a letter.

(4) If we assume the inquiry is directed to the appropriate center and the communication link is such that there is good understanding by both parties involved, a wealth of valuable information, opinions and insights may be readily assembled. Given the complexity and interrelationships in today's technology, this is one of the principal functions of an information center.

(5) Preparation of reports is a common characteristic of all information centers, as are such other services as preparing bibliographies, answering inquiries and providing consultation. Other information outlets, as SDI and a periodic publication (journal, newsletter, etc.) are much less common.

(6) In a center of any size, mechanization of the data base in some form (e.g., computer retrievable) is essential to an effective operation.

(7) At the present time all but a few centers provide their services at no charge — if they provide them at all. Charging schemes are under consideration in at least two of the seven other centers which responded to this question, and due to its inherent logic can be expected to become more commonplace in the future.

(8) The services of a majority of the centers are available to all comers, although an individual is somewhat less likely (61%) to be served than either a university or private industry (77%), both of which are second to government contractors (85%). The lower service eligibility of other government agencies (70%) may reflect a reluctance on the part of one agency to do work for another.

References

(1) President's Science Advisory Committee, "Science Information and Government," January 10, 1962.

(2) "A Study of Environmental Quality Information Programs in the Federal Government," Report of the SEQUIP Committee to the Office of Science and Technology, May 1971 (soon to be released).

(3) Z. Combs, D.K. Truby, and J.R. Buchanan, "Directory of Environmental Information Sources," ORNL-EIS-71-5, October 1971.

(4) "Directory of Selected Specialized Information Services," Ad Hoc Forum of Scientific and Technical Information Analysis Center Managers, Directors, and Professional Analysis, CONF 651131, November 1965.

(5) "Directory of USAEC Information Analysis Centers," January 1972, USAEC.

Key for Information Centers Listed in Tables 1 and 5

No.	Name	Agency	Mission (from SEQUIP report)
13	Division of Health Effects Research	EPA	Effects of air pollution on health
14	Division of Pesticide Comm. Studies	EPA	Effects of pesticides on health
15	Division of Planning and Research	Dept. of Int.	Compile outdoor recreation projects
17	Ecological Info. and Analysis Center (EIAC)	BMI-COL	Bioenvironmental and ecological information
18	Ecological Sciences Information Center	ORNL-AEC	Environmental pollutants in various ecosystems
19	Ecosystem Analysis Info. Center	ORNL-NSF	Information on biomed program
21	Emergency Operations Control Center (EOCC)	NAPCA	Provide info. to local authorities on air pollution episodes
22	Engineer Agency for Resources Inventories	Army	Environmental Planning documents
24	Environmental Hygiene Agency	Army	Support Army preventive medicine program
25	Environmental Information System	ORNL-NSF	Biblio. references and data on environmental information
26	Toxicology Information Response Center	ORNL-NIH	A response center on the hazards to man due to charcoals
27	Environmental Patent Priority Program Information	Patent	Priority processing of environmental patents
28	Environmental Pollution Effects on Aquatic Resources Program	NOAA	Ecological info. on the Columbia River and Puget Sound
29	Environmental and Radiological Health Laboratories	Air Force	Provide technical support for Air Force missions involving environment
30	Environmental Science Information Center	NOAA	Supervises NOAA's environmental information
31	Environmental Systems Applications Center	Indiana Univ.-NASA	Provide environmental information services
32	Environmental Technical Applications Center	Air Force	Provide environmental data
33	Eutrophication Information Program	Univ. of Wisconsin	Provide info. on eutrophication of inland bodies of water
34	Flora North America Program	Smithsonian	Info. on vascular plants of N.A.
37	Information Center for Internal Exposure	ORNL-AEC	Estimation of dose due to internally deposited radionuclides
38	Health Sciences Info. Center	NIH	Provide info. for program planning
40	Medical Lit. Analysis & Retrieval System (MEDLARS)	NIH	All information on medicine and related fields
45	National Meteorological Center	NOAA	Analysis and prediction of air pollution potential
51	Nuclear Safety Information Center	ORNL-AEC	Info. on safe design and operation of nuclear facilities and handling nuclear materials
61	Smithsonian Inst. Library	Smithsonian	Characteristics of biota
62	Smithsonian Science Information Exchange	Smithsonian	Info. on all types of current and basic research
65	Technical Information Service Center	AEC	All national and international nuclear science literature
66	Technical Information Service Branch	NIOSH-HEW	Information on occupational health and safety
68	Toxicology Information Program	NIH-HEW	A response center on hazards to man due to chemicals

Table 1: Characteristics of 29 Biological IAC's Listed in SEQUIP Report Based upon a Survey August-September 1972

| | Users Served | | | | | | Information Provided | | | | | | | | | | | | |
No.	Indiv.	Univ.	Indus.	Govt. Contr.	Govt. Agency	Other	Gen. Biblio.	Spec. Biblio.	Ans. Inq.	Con-sult.	Re-ports	Data	SDI	News-letter	Other	Documents per Year	Staff	Charge	Brochure Provided
14	Yes	Yes	Yes	Yes	Yes		Yes	Yes	Yes	No	Yes	No	No	No	Yes	3,000	4		Yes
17	Yes	No	Yes	Yes	Yes	Yes	Yes	Yes	Yes	Yes	Yes	Yes	No	No	No	2,000	2	No	No
21	No	No	Yes	No	Yes	No	No	No	Yes	Yes	Yes	Yes	No	No	No		5		No
24	Yes	Yes	Yes	Yes	Yes	Yes	No	No	No	Yes	Yes	Yes	No	No	No	100	10	No	No
26	Yes	Yes	Yes	Yes	Yes		Yes	Yes	No	Yes	Yes	Yes	No	No	No		6.5	*	Yes
27	No	No	No	No	No	No	No	No	No	No	No	No	No	No					No
32	Referred request to higher authorities for reply.																		
33	Yes	Yes	Yes	Yes	Yes	Yes	Yes	Yes	Yes	Yes	Yes	Yes	No	No	No	400	4	No	No
38	Yes	Yes	Yes	No	Yes	Yes	Yes	Yes	Yes	Yes	Yes	No	No	Yes	No		4		No
40	No	Yes	No	Yes	No	No	Yes	Yes	Yes	Yes	Yes	No	Yes	No	No	700,000	10	No	Yes
45	No	Yes	Yes	No	Yes	Yes	Yes	Yes	Yes	Yes	Yes	Yes	No	Yes	No	13,000	60		No
51	Yes	Yes	Yes	Yes	Yes	Yes	Yes	Yes	Yes	Yes	Yes	Yes	Yes	Yes	Yes	15,000	12	*	Yes
61	No	No	No	No	No	No	Yes	Yes	Yes	Yes	No	No	Yes	No	Yes	18,000	52	No	No
62	Yes	Yes	Yes	No	No	No	Yes	Yes	Yes	Yes	Yes	Yes	Yes	Yes	Yes		32	Yes	No
68	Yes	Yes	Yes	Yes	Yes	Yes	Yes	Yes	Yes	Yes	Yes	Yes	Yes	Yes	Yes	100,000			Yes

Requests to this center are processed by the Toxicology Information Response Center, 26 above.

*Under consideration.

Note: Numbers 13, 19, 25, 29, 30 and 31 are not included in the table because they were not contacted. Numbers 15, 18, 22, 28, 34, 37, 65 and 66 did not reply.

Table 2: Users Served

Individuals	61%
Universities	77%
Industry	77%
Government Contractors	85%
Government Agencies	70%

Table 3: Information Provided

General Bibliographies	77%
Specific Bibliographies	77%
Answer Inquiries	85%
Provide Consultation	85%
Prepare Reports	92%
Develop Data	54%
SDI (selective dissemination of information)	30%
Publications	30%
Other	30%

Table 4: Information Resources

Documents per Year		Staff		Documents per Year Staff	Charge
Range	Mean	Range	Mean		
100 to 700,000	~10,000	2 to 60	10	1,000	92% free

Table 5: Survey of the 27 Biological IAC's from SEQUIP Report

No.	Date Sent	Date Received	Span	Postage	Information Provided	Brochure	Sources Provided	Requested Identified	Opinions Provided	Evaluation	Response to 2nd Survey
13	8/4	8/9	5	Govt. 1st	7 documents and biblio.	No	Good	Yes	Outside scope	A-	-
14	8/4	8/21	17	Govt. Air	8 documents and few biblio.	No	Good	Yes	No	A-	No
15	8/10	-								E	No
17	8/9	8/15	6	8¢, 1st	Biblio. of 3 listings	No	No	Yes	No	C-	Yes
18	8/9	8/22	13	24¢, 1st	Biblio. of 15 listings	Yes	No	Yes	Outside scope	B	No
19	8/10	-								E	-
21	8/9	9/6	28	Govt. 1st	3 documents, 1 biblio.	Yes	3 Good	1 Good	No	A-	Yes
22	8/9	8/15	6	Govt. 1st	Letter with brochure	Yes	No	No	No	D	No
24	8/10	8/24	14	Govt. Air	Brochure, 1 docu.	Yes	1 Fair	Yes	Referred	B-	No
25	8/10	8/21	11	24¢, 3rd	Several biblio. and articles	No	Fair	Yes	Specific referrals	B-	-
26	8/9	8/24	15	32¢, 24¢, 8¢, 1st	Several biblio. and comments	Yes	Yes	Yes	Yes	A	No
27	8/9	8/25	16	Govt. 1st	List of patents	No	No	Yes	Outside scope	B-	Yes
28	8/8	-								E	No
29	8/10	8/17	7	Govt. 1st G	1 report	No	1 Poor	No	Outside scope	C-	-
30	8/10	8/21	11	Govt. 1st	2 biblio.	No	No	Fair	Referred	B-	-
31	8/10	8/21	11	37¢, 3rd	Brochures	Yes	A charge for services			X	-

(continued)

Table 5: (continued)

No.	Date Sent	Date Received	Span	Postage	Information Provided	Brochure	Sources Requested Provided	Identified	Opinions Provided	Evaluation	Response to 2nd Survey
32	8/9	8/29	20	Govt. 1st	Ref. to other sources	No	No	No	No	D	Yes
33	8/8	8/15	7	8¢, 1st		No	No	No	No	C-	Yes
34	8/8	-								E	No
37	8/8	8/16	8	40¢, 1st	2 reports	Yes	2 Good	No	Partially	B-	No
38	8/9	8/17	8	Govt. 1st	1 report	No	1 Fair	No	Referred	B	Yes
40	8/9	8/17	8	40¢, 1st	Need additional information	Yes	Need additional information			Y	Yes
45	8/9	8/15	6	Govt. 1st Air	1 report	Yes	1 Good	Yes	Yes	B	Yes
61	8/9	8/31	22	Govt. 1st	Don't respond to such	No	Referred to SIE			D	Yes
62	8/10	8/15	5	44¢, Air	Brochures	Yes	A charge for services		Partially	X	Yes
65	8/10	8/18	8	Govt. 1st	3 abstracts, 3 reports	Yes	Excellent	Excellent		A	No
66	8/9	8/22	13	Govt. 1st	1 report, 1 biblio.	No	1 Good	1 Good	Yes	B	No

A = Responsive and to the issue with substantive material
B = Responded to the subject but not deeply
C = Response an apparent formality, some useful material
D = Trivia
E = No reply
X = Charge for services
Y = Wanted additional information

APPENDIX A

Text of Cover Letter Sent to SEQUIP Centers

The Nuclear Safety Information Center was established by the U.S. Atomic Energy Commission to serve the nuclear community by collecting, storing, evaluating, and disseminating information relating to the safe operation of nuclear facilities. Although the technical scope of NSIC has always included a nominal effort on the consequences of effluent releases from nuclear power plants, as of four years ago our efforts on environmental effects were significantly increased. The complete technical scope of NSIC is shown on the attachment hereto. Over 30% of NSIC's total effort (11 technical man-years) is allocated to the site and environmental categories (Nos. 2, 14, 15, 16, 19, 20 and 21) listed on the attachment.

For our users, we frequently undertake special bibliographic searches as well as undertake to provide technical answers to specific questions. In view of the detailed specialized knowledge required to respond to many of the questions, we are frequently confronted with the need of referring some inquiries to more specialized information sources. However, before doing so on a routine basis, I would first like to ascertain from you the nature of the response that such a referral to you could be expected to elicit. This will enable us to best respond to the inquiries we receive and to ascertain that the user is directed to the best information available for his need. It would permit us to direct to you only those potential users that you are in a position to accommodate.

Toward that end, I have prepared the enclosed brief questionnaire, which I hope you would be so kind as to fill out and return, together with some descriptive literature on your program. For your information and use, I am enclosing a brochure of NSIC.

Note: The NSIC Environmental Questionnaire is reproduced on the following page.

NSIC Environmental Questionnaire

		Yes	No
(1)	Does the scope of your activity fall in or include any of the following information categories?		
	Siting of Nuclear Facilities	___	___
	Radionuclide Release and Movement in the Environment	___	___
	Environmental Surveys, Monitoring and Radiation Dose Measurements	___	___
	Meteorological Considerations	___	___
	Radiation Dose to Man from Radioactivity Release to the Environment	___	___
	Effects of Thermal Modifications of Ecological Systems	___	___
	Effects of Radionuclides and Ionizing Radiation on Ecological Systems	___	___
(2)	Do you provide information to the following users?		
	Private Citizens	___	___
	Universities	___	___
	Private Industry	___	___
	Government Contractors	___	___
	Government Agencies	___	___
	Other (explain)	___	___
(3)	What type of information do you provide?		
	General Bibliographic Searches	___	___
	Special Bibliographic Searches	___	___
	Answers to Technical Inquiries	___	___
	Consultation	___	___
	Reports	___	___
	Data	___	___
	Selective Dissemination of Information	___	___
	Newsletter	___	___
	Other (explain)	___	___

(4) What is the size of your information base and equivalent full-time technical personnel?

We access approximately ____ documents per year.
We have a technical staff of ____ equivalent full-time people.

(5) Which, if any, of the above services to you charge for and how much? Please explain.

This questionnaire was completed by _____ on _____
for _____
(give complete name and address of center)

APPENDIX B

Text of Letter Requesting Specific Information

This letter is a request for information with which I understand your Information Center is involved. First as regards my interest and need, I am Assistant Research Director of Environmental Engineering and Research Corporation (EERC) of Memphis. Since the first of this year I have been on leave of absence to do work on my doctorate at the University of Tennessee. My thesis work is supported by EERC because of its potential industrial applications in the control of liquid effluents.

I learned from a colleague that you were Director of the Environmental Science Information Center which was established to collect and evaluate scientific and technical information for the National Oceanic and Atmospheric Administration and outside groups, and that you very probably would have information of value to me by current investigation. I am particularly interested in the following:

(1) Effects of large municipal sewage effluents re-
     leased in or near the ocean on aquatic plants
     and marine animals.

(2) Research conducted during the last three years
     on methods of upgrading these effluents.

I would appreciate receiving a current bibliography on the above topics from your information files, as well as your own evaluation of the most effective methods of reducing BOD in effluents from paper mills. To be of greatest value, I would need to receive this information by August 25.

In addition, I would like to get a description (e.g., brochure, circular, etc.) of your Information Center. I appreciate your cooperation and assistance in this matter.

SCIENTIFIC AND TECHNICAL PRIMARY PUBLICATIONS
CARRYING ENVIRONMENTAL INFORMATION

D.H. Michael Bowen
Managing Editor,
ENVIRONMENTAL SCIENCE & TECHNOLOGY
American Chemical Society
Washington, D.C.

My task today is to try to describe to you the range of primary publications that carry scientific and technical information in the environmental field, and to give you some idea of the type of information, level of understanding needed, cost and availability of these publications.

This task has been considerably eased by the valiant efforts of the organizers of this symposium, who have tried their very best to ensure that there is not too much overlap between what I will say and what will be presented by other speakers at the symposium. The task, however, is still a difficult one, for several reasons. First, "environmental" information covers a multitude of sins; much scientific information is not of direct and obvious environmental significance, but may be indirectly (or at a date much later than initial publication) of very great significance. Second, there are many publications that carry information that is environmental and technical in nature, but which are nevertheless not normally considered as environmentally related publications.

When you consider these two reasons, you will immediately appreciate how important is the role of secondary and abstracting publications, and of information services, and how vital it is that these publications and services have as extensive a data base as possible. Bernard Rosenthal, who will speak to you later, will describe these secondary publications. I shall confine myself to primary scientific and technical publications.

Now, what do I mean by "primary"? For the sake of simplicity, and at the risk of oversimplification, I mean a publication that publishes information written by the generator of the information, or written by him and rewritten by someone else. By this definition, newspapers, for example, are not primary publications, nor for obvious reasons, are secondary publications which abstract or extract pieces from something that has already been published. By this definition, too, parts of my own publication — ES&T — do not qualify as primary, since these parts contain accounts of technical work written by people other than the originators. There are many technical and scientific publications, though, that contain both primary and secondary material, and I shall consider these for the purpose of this talk as being primary.

At the outset, I must confess that it is impossible to be completely comprehensive in an area of such variety and magnitude as environmentally related scientific and technical publications. So, if I omit reference to some publications in my talk, or in the supplementary material that is distributed — and I am sure to do so — I beg your indulgence and take all responsibility. I have tried to be as unbiased as possible in selecting publications to mention; I have selected those known to me that I believe will best illustrate the types of publications that are available.

There are many ways to categorize publications in the environmental field. One very simple way is to look at them as very old ones and very new ones. The old ones are exemplified by those in the field of public health, which have been publishing for 20 years or more. New ones are arriving on the scene almost daily, in response to two factors:

(1)   the tremendous explosion in public awareness of environmental problems; and
(2)   the just-beginning explosion in scientific and technical studies of environmentally related problems and the consequent need on the part of scientists for a publications outlet.

The number of new publications in this field is truly astounding. At a conservative guess, 30 or so have started up in the last five years. And although many of these could be, perhaps unfairly, categorized as "bandwagon" publications, many do serve a useful purpose in that they provide an outlet that relieves the older publications of a crushing volume of material.

Even so, sheer proliferation has of course made it very much more difficult to select publications to which to subscribe, or even to read regularly. Really the only people to benefit in any concrete way from this proliferation are the publishers of secondary publications! For them, the information explosion has been a boon. To the extent that secondary publications can digest the mass of material in primary publications and supply it in useful form, the increase in the number of primary publications may or may not be a crushing burden to the seeker of environmental information. Mr. Rosenthal will tell how secondary services are trying to cope.

A more useful way to categorize scientific and technical publications is as "overtly environmental" and "incidentally environmental." It is the first group that we are primarily concerned with but, as I hope to show, the second group is very important.

For the purpose of this talk, I have broken down each of the two groups into the following types of publications: scientific journals, technical journals, trade press, general magazines and nonscientific journals. There is a certain arbitrariness in this sort of a breakdown, but there is also some logic as I shall shortly show.

OVERTLY ENVIRONMENTAL PUBLICATIONS

Scientific Journals

This group represents the basic current literature in the field. A scientist wishing to publish work that is fundamental in nature and related to an environmental problem would most probably (but not necessarily) approach one of these publications. One of the distinguishing features of publications in this group is that papers are reviewed before publication by several scientists other than the author. This procedure — often known as "peer judgment" — has its disadvantages but it does tend to ensure that anything that is published is scientifically correct and that conclusions are supportable by the evidence presented. In a field as replete with controversy as "environment" this is an important point.

Another distinguishing feature of scientific journals is that they are written "by experts for experts" and consequently there is little or no effort made to make articles in them understandable by anyone not extremely conversant with the particular subject. For instance, a degree in chemistry is not always sufficient equipment to enable one to read and fully understand every paper in my own publication, ES&T. In general, a high degree of proficiency in physical sciences, biological sciences and mathematics may be needed to get anything at all out of most of the publications in this group. This is, of course, true for the whole of the scientific literature, and not just for that part of it that is "overtly environmental."

As a group these publications are, in addition to being technically advanced, moderately expensive (by that I mean an annual subscription may range from $10 to $50 a year), usually appear monthly, are easily available if you can afford the subscription price but otherwise are to be found only in technical libraries. Few public libraries subscribe to these publications and I have yet to see any of them on the newsstand.

In summation, they contain information that is most likely to be accurate, within carefully stated bounds, but not everyone can read them. A partial list of "overtly environmental" scientific journals is given in Table 1 at the end of this chapter.

Technical Journals

There really isn't too much difference between these journals and the purely scientific journals I just discussed. Perhaps the main difference is that the technical journals are at a lower level of technical difficulty than the scientific journals. Even so, they generally require expertise to be read intelligently. Papers in technical journals also are reviewed by outside reviewers, as are papers in scientific journals, with the same net result — some assurance that published papers have a sort of "Good Housekeeping Seal of Approval" from the technical community.

The technical journals I have listed in Table 2 are, as it happens, all published by professional associations, and each is aimed primarily at practitioners of some rather specific aspect of environment, such as water treatment or air pollution control. These journals are therefore primarily also in the "by experts for experts" category, but their more down-to-earth technical level makes them somewhat easier to read than scientific journals.

These journals, too, tend to be expensive; the Journal of the Air Pollution Control Association costs $75 per year for nonmembers of the Association. But they are truly excellent reference sources on some subjects, for instance the feasibility of different types of pollution control methods, and could be helpful to diligent laymen, as well as to the professionals for whom they are primarily intended. These publications are usually available in technical libraries, seldom in public libraries, and never to my knowledge on newsstands. There are no bars to subscribing beyond the rather steep subscription prices.

Trade Press

Trade publications are usually characterized by relatively large circulations, relatively low technical difficulty, and modest subscription price. They are published by commercial publishers whose main goal must necessarily be to make a profit. Key to the viability of these publications is a lively market for products and services which can be made the subject of display advertising. Since advertisers are interested in large audiences consisting of people who have both the need and the means to buy their products, the publisher needs to guarantee that large audience. Often this is achieved through "controlled circulation," a device by which suitable "qualified" subscribers pay nothing to receive the publication. Those whose jobs do not qualify them may nevertheless subscribe to trade publications; the annual subscription is usually around $10.

Because of the economics of this type of publication, there tends to be more of them in the fields where there is a sizeable dollar market: water and waste treatment is such an area.

I think it fair to say that trade publications in general vary considerably in quality, and "overtly environmental" trade publications are no exception. The best of them are really very good, but the fact that information is usually not subject to technical review (except inasmuch as the editors exert technical judgment) works against their overall stature and credibility. The worst of them can be quite bad and unreliable sources of technical information.

These publications are commonly to be found in technical libraries, and some are found in public libraries (The American City is one that springs to mind). They are easy to read, and this fact alone does commend them to anyone who does not have the training or education to read the more technically advanced journals, subject to the caveats I have mentioned. Trade publications are listed in Table 3.

General Magazines

This is a category that has grown in size, in fact grown from nothing, in the past few years. These magazines are aimed at the laymen, or "concerned citizen," and are mentioned here because they do sometimes contain primary information. Technical level is almost uniformly low. The best (in my opinion) is the magazine <u>Environment</u>.

As a group, they are not overly reliable sources of information, and they tend to go off on tangents (such as organic burial), but they are designed to be readable. Although subscription costs are quite low —$10 per year is the norm — it is my feeling that many are struggling financially and we may see considerable attrition over the next year or two. Public libraries often have these publications; <u>Environment</u> seems to have been particularly successful in this regard. These magazines are listed in Table 4.

Nonscientific Journals

The nature of the environmental field is such that technical information is at its very core, so that it is hardly possible to discuss an environmental problem without bringing science into the picture. In their various fields, the nonscientific journals have the same strengths and weaknesses as those in the scientific and technical field, namely that the most reliable information is to be found in the least readable publication. See Table 5.

INCIDENTALLY ENVIRONMENTAL PUBLICATIONS

Because of the all-pervasive nature of environmental problems and interests, it is safe to say that nearly all scientific and technical primary publications at one time or another carry information that can be characterized as environmental. Thus, all scientific journals based on physical or biological sciences are at least potential, and usually regular, publishers of environmental information. As I mentioned previously, this is the reason why it is so important for these journals to be represented in the data base of environmental information systems and to be abstracted by secondary services.

Regular issues of such scientific journals as <u>Biochemistry</u>, <u>Separation Science</u>, <u>Analytical Chemistry</u>, to take three entirely at random, ordinarily contain several papers of environmental significance. So do the journals serving agricultural science. Since these journals are at a high technical level, however, it takes a trained specialist to dig out the information.

Technical journals and trade publications serving particular professions and segments of industry regularly carry environmental information, especially that which is pertinent to their particular interest. For example, Modern Plastics can be expected to review incinerability of plastics and the role of packaging materials in solid waste. Oil and Gas Journal, a trade publication in the petroleum field, deals on a regular basis with refinery pollution control, auto exhaust emissions and other environmental concerns of the petroleum industry. Civil Engineering and Chemical Engineering Progress — official publications of two engineering societies — also contain much technical environmental information.

Environmental information — technical and primary in nature — can be found in almost any issue of Scientific American, and even in the business monthly, Fortune.

The rough guides given above for the various types of publications should be used to gauge the potential utility, cost, technical level and availability of these "incidentally environmental" publications.

To sum up briefly, environmental information is to be found in a staggering number of primary scientific and technical publications. That number is certainly in the hundreds.

The most reliable information (in the scientific sense) is to be found in publications that are the most expensive, the least available, and the most difficult to read and understand. Conversely, publications that are inexpensive, easy to read, and easily available tend to sacrifice accuracy and scientific objectivity. This may be a generalization, but it is sufficiently true to pose very real problems for anyone who is not technically trained and who wishes to mine the very rich ore to be found in the scientific literature.

Explanations of Column Headings in Tables 1 Through 5

Cost

Annual subscription in U.S. Those affiliated with society or association generally get price break. Foreign subscriptions cost more; institutional subscriptions usually cost more than individual.

C.C. means "controlled circulation" — free subscription to "qualified readers." Those not qualified must pay.

Aimed At

The primary audience for whom publication is edited. Publications sometimes use jargon and special terms which only its primary audience can understand.

Technical Level

Low: can probably be read by educated laymen.

Moderate: technical training may be necessary to understand some or all articles.

High: specialized technical training essential to understand articles.

Availability

Indication of whether available on newsstands, in public libraries, technical libraries, or so specialized or to be available only in some technical libraries.

Note: These lists are not claimed to be totally comprehensive. They should be considered only as a guide to technical literature and as indicative of different types of publications.

Table 1: Scientific Journals

Title	Publisher (Year of Appearance)	Frequency	Cost	Aimed At	Technical Level	Availability
Environmental Science & Technology	American Chem. Soc. (1967)	Monthly with annual directory	$9.00	Env. Profs.	Low-High	Technical libraries, some public libraries
Environmental Pollution	Elsevier (1970)	Quarterly	$15.60	Env. Res.	High	Technical libraries
Water Research	Pergamon Press (1967)	Monthly	$100.00	Water Sci.	High	Technical libraries
Water Resources Research	Am. Geophys. Union (1965)	Bimonthly	$20.00	Water Supply Profs.	High	Technical libraries
Bulletin of Environmental Contamination and Toxicology	Springer-Verlag (1966)	Bimonthly	$28.00	Prof. Toxicols.	High	Technical libraries
Atmospheric Environment	Pergamon Press (1967)	Monthly	$60.00	Air Pol. Profs.	High	Technical libraries
Environmental Letters	Marcel Dekker (1971)	8/year	$40.00	Env. Res.	High	Technical libraries
Journal of Environmental Sciences	Institute of Env. Sciences (1958)	Bimonthly	$12.00	Env. Res.	High	Technical libraries

Table 2: Technical Journals

Title	Publisher (Year of Appearance)	Frequency	Cost	Aimed At	Technical Level	Availability
Journal Water Pollution Control Federation	Water Pol. Control Federation (1928)	Monthly with 2 extra issues	$35.00	Water Pol. Profs.	Moderate-High	Technical libraries
Journal of the Air Pollution Control Assn.	Air. Pol. Control Assn. (1951)	Monthly	$25.00 to nonprofit lib. & indiv.	Water Supply Profs.	Moderate-High	Technical libraries
Journal of American Water Works Assn.	Amer. Water Works Assn. (1914)	Monthly	$20.00	Water Supply Profs.	Moderate	Technical libraries
Journal of the Sanitary Engineering Div. (ASCE)	Amer. Society of Civil Engineers				Moderate-High	Technical libraries
Journal of Environmental Health	Nat. Env. Health Assn. (1938)	Bimonthly	$ 8.00	Public Health Profs.	Low-Moderate	Technical libraries

Table 3: Trade Press

Title	Publisher (Year of Appearance)	Frequency	Cost	Aimed At	Technical Level	Availability
Industrial Wastes		Bimonthly	C.C. or $10.00	Ind. Waste Engrs. & Off.	Low-Moderate	Some technical libraries
Water & Sewage Works	Scranton Publ. Co. (1890)	Monthly	$7.50	Munic. Water & Waste Eng. & Off.	Low-Moderate	Some technical libraries
Effluent & Water Treatment Journal (British)	Thunderbird Enterprises (1961)	Monthly	$15.00	Munic. Water & Waste Eng. & Off.	Low-Moderate	Some technical libraries
Water & Wastes Engineering	Dun-Donnelley (1964)	Monthly	C.C. or $6.00	Water Supply Profs.	Low	Some technical libraries
Industrial Water Engineering	Target Communic. (1963)	Bimonthly	C.C. or $10.00	Water Supply Profs.	Low-Moderate	Some technical libraries
Pollution Engineering	Technical Publ. (1969)	Monthly	C.C. or $12.00	Ind. Eng. Management	Moderate	Technical libraries
Waste Age	3 Sons Publ. Co. (1970)	Bimonthly	C.C. or $10.00	Solid Waste Profs.	Low	?
Environmental Pollution Management (British)	The Nat'l. Mag. Co. (1971)	Monthly	C.C. only	Ind. Management	Low	?
The American City	Buttenheim Publ. Co. (1909)	Monthly	C.C. or $15.00	Munic. Off.	Low	Technical libraries Many public lib.
Solid Waste Management	RRJ Publ. Co. (1958)	Monthly	$6.00	Solid Waste Profs.	Low	Technical libraries

Table 4: General Magazines

Title	Publisher (Year) of Appearance	Frequency	Cost	Aimed At	Technical Level	Availability
Ecology Today	Ecological Dimensions (1970)	Bimonthly	$6.00	Concerned Laymen	Low	Mail subscription Some public libraries
The Ecologist (British)	The Ecologist Ltd. (1970)	Monthly	$12.00	Concerned Laymen	Low	Mail subscription
Clean Air (British)	Nat. Soc. for Clean Air (1929)	Quarterly	$3.50	Concerned Laymen and Profs.	Low	Some libraries
Environmental Quality Magazine	Env. Awareness Assoc. (1970)	Monthly	$10.00	Concerned Environmentalists "Ecofreaks"	Low	Newsstands ($1)
Environment	Comm. for Env. Inf. (1958)	10 issues per year	$10.00	Intelligent Laymen	Low-Moderate	Technical libraries Many public libraries

Table 5: Nonscientific Journals

Title	Publisher (Year) of Appearance	Frequency	Cost	Aimed At	Technical Level	Availability
Environmental Affairs	Boston Coll. Env. Law Center (1971)	Quarterly	$15.00	Interdisciplinary Audience of Profs.	Low-Moderate	?

SECONDARY TECHNICAL AND SCIENTIFIC JOURNALS

Bernard D. Rosenthal
President, Pollution Abstracts, Inc.

There has been a substantial increase in the number of primary
sources and publications, i.e., journals, books, technical reports,
symposia, academic literature and government documents, both
domestic and foreign, that contain information about the environment and related subjects. The volume of literature in number of
sources and diversity of content has led to selective dissemination
of information (SDI) on most aspects of environmental information.

The secondary publication is the SDI link for a user's specific or un-
refined information need as he confronts thousands of primary information options. General examples of secondary publications
are reviewed in this paper. No evaluation is made of their content
in scope or presentation. An attempt is made to highlight the variety of formats, the diversity of sources and to offer the user a guide
for evaluating secondary publications.

The value of a secondary publication depends in part on the user's
understanding of his own needs and objectives. He should understand the objective of a specific secondary publication. Value to
the user depends upon:

(a) how specific the information must be,
(b) the scope of the information required,
(c) lapse or lag time from publication date of the original
       document until its appearance in a secondary journal,
(d) the expertise of writing technique,
(e) ease of use and reference,

(f)   availability of original document retrieval service,
(g)   whether the information base can be manipulated to satisfy user needs more defined than the presentation in the secondary journal, and
(h)   the publishing frequency of the secondary journal.

Also, is there sufficient information used from the secondary source to justify its cost? Other values relate to the number of original source documents utilized by the secondary publication, unique subjects covered, and whether foreign documents are included.

Essentially, the secondary publication prior to publishing must (a) collect information by acquisition or request, (b) prepare bibliographic reference for each original source cited, and (c) abstract and index, if each mode is part of the publication's character. There are adjuncts and alternatives to secondary publication services. These may exist within or outside the services of a publication. These would include magnetic tapes, microform service, computer printouts, duplication of the original full text source documents (maintaining copyright restrictions), on-line computer availability and alerting services for early awareness of primary source information.

Secondary journals often include an abstract of an original document. An abstract is a condensation of information and content. The abstract is used as a screening medium to assist the user in deciding whether the original document should be reviewed in its entirety. Some abstracts include data, observations, facts, conclusions, or a mixture of each. Some take the form of being informative; others are explanatory, comparative or selective.

There are several basic standard reference or access points included in secondary publications. These include:

(1)   reference code to each reference or citation and title of article;
(2)   author identification;
(3)   author affiliation;
(4)   primary publication source;
(5)   analytics, including date of primary publication, number of pages cited, page references in original document, referrals to charts and other unique information.

Each secondary publication has its own method of subarrangement.

The user must learn the different arrangements and how to use each most effectively. The subdivisions include indexes with regular issues, annual indexes and possibly cumulative indexes.

Search vocabulary is perhaps the most unique characteristic of each secondary publication. It may also be the most frustrating for the user. Secondary journals have no common thesaurus. They are not common to each other nor are they wholly common to government vocabulary. A descriptor or keyword essential for searching one secondary source may not be relative to searching another secondary source on the same general subject.

The lack of compatibility in arrangement, order of bibliographic data and vocabulary exists within government publications on environmental information as well as in private secondary publications.

What follows is a brief overview of certain publications and sources in the secondary field as they relate to environmental subjects.

Air Pollution Abstracts: Includes more than 1,200 "core" domestic and foreign journals. Implemented by Air Pollution Technical Information Center (APTIC), now part of the Office of Technical Information and Publications, Office of Air Programs (OAP), Environmental Protection Agency (EPA). Covers chemical, physical and biological effects of air pollution, and the data on air pollution control.

Selected Water Resources Abstracts: Reviews current reports and articles on water-related aspects of the life, physical and social sciences; and the conservation, control, use, management and other engineering and legal aspects of water. Covers water pollution, water lay, ground water, lakes and estuaries, water yield, watershed protection, waste treatment, water demand, hydraulics and soil mechanics. Compiled by the U.S. Department of the Interior. Available from National Technical Information Service (NTIS).

Solid Waste Information Retrieval System (SWIRS): Offers information concerning current research and technological developments in the solid waste management field throughout the world. Coverage includes literature published since 1964. Available from Environmental Protection Agency.

Transportation Noise Bulletin: Presents abstracts of reports and resumes of research projects dealing with transportation noise. Compiled from records of Transportation Noise Research Information

Service (TNRIS), National Academy of Sciences, Washington, D.C.

Ascatopics of Institute for Scientific Information (ISI): Titles, authors and journal citations on environmental sciences that include air pollution, effects, source and control; biological waste treatment, chemical residues related to soil contamination, food and beverages; noise control, solid wastes, water pollution and other environmental areas. Available from ISI, Philadelphia, Pa.

Medical Literature Analysis & Retrieval System (MEDLARS): From Medlar data the Toxicity Bibliography is produced. Emphasis on adverse effects of toxicity and poisoning of drugs and chemicals, pesitcides and other environmental pollutants. Available from Government Printing Office, Washington, D.C.

Abstracts on Health Effects of Environmental Pollutants: Prepared in conjunction with Biological Abstracts and with BA's BioResearch Index. Emphasis on pesticides and other environmental pollutants. Publication started January 1972. Developed by Toxicology Information Program, National Institutes of Health. Available from Bio-Sciences Information Service of Biological Abstracts, Philadelphia, Pa.

Selected References on Environmental Quality As It Relates to Health: Citations only. Prepared by MEDLARS. Available from Government Printing Office.

Environmental Information Access: Indexing, abstracting and information retrieval service that covers published and nonprint information on the environment and related fields. Provides subscribers with an overview of some 450 periodicals, newspapers and other publications; research and retrieval services are available. From Environmental Information Center of Ecology Forum, New York. Annual index available.

Pollution Abstracts: Indexing, abstracting and information retrieval service. Covers worldwide literature, published and noncirculated, with about 10,000 abstracts annually from 19,000 books, journals, papers, government documents. References from over 11,500 authors. Annual cumulative index. Translations included. Reference by citation number, author, source document and Keytalpha (rotating keywords). Air, water, solid waste, land, noise, fresh water, sewage treatment, contracts and patents. General and technical coverage. Available from Pollution Abstracts, La Jolla, Calif.

There are numerous secondary publications worldwide in certain environmental fields. For example, Informatics, Inc., in a project for EPA's Noise Abatement and Control Division, found 35 secondary publications involved with abstracting and indexing, United States and foreign, noise information.

There are 46 services worldwide who deal with abstracting and indexing of water resources or water technology, based on Abstracting Services, Science and Technology, The Hague, FID, 1969, Vol. #1.

There is no single reference source to all the secondary sources that relate to environmental literature.

The secondary publication has significant value to the user. It (1) alerts the user to the availability of the vast number of primary source documents; (2) exposes this information to the user without requiring the purchase of original source documents; (3) lets the user's rationale determine the importance of the primary material; (4) allows the user to "track" specialized topics, publications, authors; and (5) keeps the user alert to changes in the state of the art of subjects of specific interest.

There will probably be more SDI of environmental information. It will be a result of increased demand for more specific coverage of environmental subjects. The performance of SDI will come from either existing secondary publications or from new publications. The results will be more proliferation of environmental information in the secondary field.

ENVIRONMENTAL LITIGATION
AS A SOURCE OF ENVIRONMENTAL INFORMATION

Victor J. Yannacone, Jr.
Yannacone & Yannacone
Patchogue, New York

Litigation has been called civilization's alternative to revolution, and certainly environmental litigation represents a substantial source of tested and evaluated environmental information of use to scientists, engineers, legislators, officials of regulatory agencies, business and industrial managers, and the general public.

Within the Anglo-American system of jurisprudence, the bulk of the substantive law is contained in serially promulgated, chronologically published reports of judicial opinions generally grouped for the purpose of binding according to the Court which renders the decision. The entire set of these published judicial opinions and decisions makes up the body of what is traditionally referred to as the Common Law. Over the last one hundred years several attempts have been made by private publishers and government agencies to index and abstract these decisions, and since great weight is placed upon the doctrine of *stare decisis*, within the Anglo-American system of jurisprudence, the need to locate particular precedent becomes more important and more difficult as the elements of the set of all judicial opinions and decisions increase in number.

The generally accepted index and abstract services utilized by the legal profession to search the vast body of Common Law have been the product of private enterprise in the field of legal publishing, and range from the straightforward Sheppard's Citations through the Key Number System of the West Publishing Company to the heavily editorially dependent Total Client Service Library of the Lawyers Cooperative Publishing Company.

While there seems to be a movement towards assembling the entire data base for that particular area of legal concern now generally designated Environmental Law in some form suitable for computer assisted search and retrieval, consideration of the origin of the phrase "Environmental Law" immediately demonstrates the difficulty of defining the data base.

Although much of the effort of the participants in the National Environmental Information Symposium and the organizations and institutions they represent has been directed toward serving the needs of legislators, administrative agencies and practitioners in certain areas of Environmental Law, environmental litigation has been largely overlooked as a primary source of environmental information. In order to properly evaluate the substantial environmental information resource represented by environmental litigation, some consideration must be given to the litigation process itself.

One of the principle characteristics of Anglo-American litigation is the adversary nature of the process, which generally commences with service of a document setting forth a claim of right and seeking some legal remedy. Litigation is essentially a dialectic process. In a criminal or quasi-criminal proceeding, the party charging that a crime has been committed (usually the People of the United States or the People of an individual State, acting as the Sovereign) has the burden of proving that all the elements of the crime have been committed by the party charged, and that burden must be sustained beyond all reasonable doubt. In civil cases, or in the general run of administrative agency proceedings, the burden is on the party seeking relief to establish the right to the relief sought by a fair preponderance of the substantial credible evidence.

A trial is conducted in an essentially linear fashion. The party with the burden of proof generally presents data or other demonstrable evidence in support of the allegations of the complaint or petition. The representative of the adverse party then tests the testimony or evidence offered against three criteria.

  Is the testimony or evidence *relevant* to the subject
      matter of the litigation?

  Is the testimony or evidence a *material* contribution to
      the evidence necessary to satisfy the burden of proof?

  Is the witness *competent* to present the testimony or
      qualified to introduce the evidence?

Following the dialectic of direct and cross-examination by the representatives of the adverse parties, the court rules, or in some cases the jury finds, whether the evidence offered is admissible; so that at the termination of any trial there is a vast body of well edited and carefully tested information which in matters of environmental litigation represents an often overlooked source of primary environmental information.

The most obvious current example is the DDT litigation. The scientific papers, studies and data ultimately accepted as evidence by the Supreme Court of the State of New York in 1966, the Court of Appeals of the State of Michigan and the United States District Court for the Western District of Michigan in 1967, the United States District Court for the Eastern District of Wisconsin and the Wisconsin Department of Natural Resources in 1968 and 1969, and the United States Environmental Protection Agency in 1972 represents the definitive compilation of the relevant, material evidence on the effects of DDT on nontarget organisms.

The dialectic process of direct and cross-examination which surrounded the admission of each item of evidence in those trials furnished the kind of editorial review that is lacking in even the most rigorous scientific journals, and furnishes decision makers with a consideration of the relevance of each item in the overall issue of the benefit-risk to the People of the United States occasioned by the continued widespread use of DDT. The dialectic process of direct and cross-examination also indicated new avenues for scientific research and inconsistencies in the existing body of scientific information on the subject at the time of trial.

There is a substantial need for a data base including the full text of Federal, state and local laws and regulations, subject to search and retrieval at the level of state of the art in computer information retrieval technology. Pending legislation, the opinions of attorneys general, legal scholars and appellate courts, together with the complete legislative history of all environmental legislation must also be included as elements of any environmental information system. The scientific information necessary to support ecologically sophisticated, environmentally responsible, socially relevant and politically feasible legislation must also be available in a form readily accessible by legislators, regulatory agencies, the Bench, the Bar, business, industry, and the public.

There is a substantial need to protect the diversity of editorial viewpoint represented by private enterprise in the area of environmental information distribution. There is a similar need to encourage the continued concern of public benefit, nonprofit corporations in the area of interdisciplinary cooperation in environmental science. The Federal government, and to a more limited, but nonetheless important extent, state and local governments, must be encouraged to improve accessibility to government generated or government sponsored data, information and publications. At the same time we must improve the access of legislators and regulatory agency personnel to available data in the private sector.

It appears that in matters of substantial public concern of an inherently controversial character, such as the benefit-risk evaluation of the continued use of certain environmental toxicants and the cost-effectiveness of public projects and certain administrative agency actions, litigation will furnish an increasingly effective and sophisticated means for resolution of issues and reduction of the data base prior to ultimate consideration by legislative bodies and regulatory agencies. It is this often overlooked function of environmental litigation, particularly in cases of benefit-risk and cost-effectiveness, which should be of increasing value to legislators and regulatory officials. Unfortunately, unless access to the data base developed during such litigation is improved, much of its value and effectiveness will be lost.

One of the most obvious results of the National Environmental Information Symposium has been the demonstration of the enormous quantity of environmental information that does exist and the continued proliferation of private and public processes contributing to the generation of more environmental information, all without general coordination and some without recognition of the inherently *multi* rather than merely *inter*disciplinary nature of Environmental Law and Environmental Science.

Just as it is essentially impossible to practice environmental law without a substantial background in environmental science, it is equally futile to attempt to organize environmental science, or more particularly classify the body of environmental information, without a considered awareness of the needs of society which lead ultimately to the legal regulation of activities having environmental impact.

APPLICATIONS OF SOCIOECONOMIC INFORMATION
TO ENVIRONMENTAL RESEARCH AND PLANNING

William B. DeVille
Director of Program Development
Gulf South Research Institute

Many years ago I read a classic 19th century book by the English archeologist, Layard, "Discoveries in the Ruins of Ninevah and Babylon."[1] More recently I was delighted to find an excerpt from Layard's account cited in a book on research writing. The excerpt, quoted here, seems very appropriate for introducing some of the points we shall be considering during this symposium. The excerpt is a letter from a Turkish official to an Englishman who had, obviously, put some very troublesome questions to the official.

> My Illustrious Friend and Joy of My Liver!
> The thing you ask of me is both difficult and useless. Although I have passed all my days in this place, I have neither counted the houses nor have I inquired into the number of the inhabitants; and as to what one person loads on his mules and the other stows away in the bottom of his ship, that is no business of mine. But above all, as to the previous history of this city, God only knows the amount of dirt and confusion that the infidels may have eaten before the coming of the sword of Islam. It were unprofitable for us to inquire into it. O my soul! O my lamb! Seek not after the things which concern thee not. Thou camest unto us and we welcomed thee: go in peace.[2]

The attitude of this 19th century Turkish official comes as a conceptual jolt to anyone who is aware of present administrative practices in Washington or any state capitol. No vital statistics! No

data on industrial productivity, labor force, or economic indicators!
No historical collation of data used for extrapolation and prediction!
Having worked a few years ago with a 20th century Turkish admin-
istrator, I can state that socioeconomic information and data furnish
grist for the mills of government in Turkey as well as in the United
States.

The attitude of some of my environmentalist friends who see little
or no reason to discuss socioeconomic information resources in the
context of attacking environmental problems hits me with a very
similar conceptual jolt. One of my friends is an ecologist who has
been studying the ecology of a small patch of grassland, paying particular attention to the field mouse population. He has gathered,
over a period of years, a vast quantity of detailed information about
the numbers of field mice, their food supplies, their relative population with respect to predators, birth and death rates under various
conditions, and so on. Several weeks ago he asked me why the
National Environmental Information Symposium was to include a
section on socioeconomic information.

Yet it seems very obvious that a great deal of the information on
field mice mentioned above is perfectly analogous to the kinds of
socioeconomic information we are discussing at this meeting, and
the relationships of analogous sets of such information to our understanding of environmental problems is very similar. Mice do not
formulate statements about environmental problems such as crowd-
ing, overpopulation, or lack of resources; but in a sense, this is precisely what the ecologist has done. We can look at our physical environment, our institutions, our population and demographic characteristics, our use or movement of resources, and many other factors
and formulate statements about our environmental problems very
like those the ecologist makes about field mice in the area of grassland.

Unlike field mice, fortunately, we can consciously analyze our problems and try to modify our behavior or our institutions in order to
solve or alleviate them. We can plan, and implement our plans. But
in order to do such planning, or to administer effectively the implementation of plans to solve environmental problems, we must ask a
great many questions about things that were anathema to our friend,
the 19th century Turkish official.

To whom can we put such questions with some hope of getting a
better response than the old Turk gave his English friend? One

answer may be to go to an information retrieval center using computerized storage and retrieval techniques. Until very recently, I was the project director of the Environmental Systems Applications Center, an environmental information center associated with a scientific and technical information center, ARAC, at Indiana University. The design, output formats, and some of our experiences at ESAC may serve to illustrate one kind of information center which attempts to service a wide variety of information requests.

The sources of information for ARAC and ESAC, or their information inputs, are periodically updated files of abstracts of reports, papers, monographs, books and other publications. Such abstract files are generated both by government and private sources.

Examples of files produced by government agencies are the NASA STAR and IAA files covering U.S. and foreign publications in the aerospace fields; U.S. Government Reports Announcements, which deals with unclassified reports from the Department of Defense as well as reports from a number of other Federal agencies; Selected Water Resources Abstracts, which is produced by the Department of Interior and deals with all phases of water quality management and water resources; Air Pollution Abstracts, produced by the Environmental Protection Agency, which covers all facets of air pollution and air pollution control; and Nuclear Sciences Abstracts, produced by the Atomic Energy Commission, which deals with all unclassified reports on radiation and atomic energy.

Examples of similar resources produced in the private sector include Chemical Abstracts Condensates, which provides worldwide coverage of the literature of chemistry and is produced by the American Chemical Society; Pollution Abstracts, which covers all facets of environmental pollution and pollution control; and Engineering Index, which provides worldwide coverage of engineering literature. These particular examples are cited because they are the most commonly used at ARAC and ESAC.

This kind of input may be called "conceptual information," to distinguish it from another kind I shall call "data." Conceptual information of this kind is an abstract or digest of the published literature. If we search a Chemical Abstracts Condensates tape in response to an information query, we are essentially providing a literature search, albeit using very sophisticated techniques.

Data input sources are quite different. An example would be the use of tapes available from the Census Bureau containing population data. A search of these tapes for a given inquiry would pull specific facts, such as the number of people of a specified sex and age group who live in some particular geographical region.

The output of information searches performed at ARAC and ESAC is almost exclusively of the conceptual information, or literature search type. If an information user needs to find out the nature and scope of the recent literature on a topic such as demographic trends in a selected area of the Midwest, ESAC might very well be able to assist him. If the topic requires some sort of correlation of demographic trends with regional transportation planning and water resources, then the odds are that ESAC will be able to provide a valuable service by rapidly surveying a very large number of literature citations, using an appropriate search strategy which will bring together the desired key terms.

The output format will be a bibliography of abstracts of the relevant literature generated by the search. Some of the major problems faced by ESAC or ARAC staff in conducting such a search should be noted here.

(1)   The request for information must be as definite as possible, particularly if the question is of a complex type which requires integrating several subtopics in the course of the search, or if the query would tend to pull a large number of citations with low relevance to the user's principal interest.

(2)   The relative quality of the literature cited in an information base is not guaranteed merely because it is there.

Both of the above problems are serious enough to require that considerable staff time be spent in analyzing the question or behavioral, social and institutional research. My component, the information storage and retrieval section, had the mission of providing information support services to the other components and planning a data management system for output of the project.

We were required to survey the support information needs of each of the research components. One of the most fascinating conclusions of this survey was that, without exception, each research component felt the need for one or more elements of socioeconomic information. As an example, an information search performed in response to inquiries on water resource planning incorporated citations on public attitudes toward water resource planning, public attitudes toward bond issues to support water resource and recreation projects, population and demographic trends in the region, and socioeconomic modeling techniques and models.

A survey of the ESAC information bases for the transportation component elicited references on the impacts of transportation development, including highway location, on tax bases and rates, land use development, the flow of goods and materials, industrial sitings, and consolidations of public school systems.

A conclusion to be drawn from this experience is that socioeconomic information is indeed relevant to systematic study of environmental planning. But having arrived at this conclusion, I should like to examine some of the blocks which tend to inhibit wider utilization of information resources, and which are in part due to the nature of services such as those developed at ESAC.

I believe that everyone in the information business agrees about some of the blocks to information use. The first big one is habit. People have not been trained to use and evaluate information services, and a request for information services from a computerized storage and retrieval system just doesn't fit the life style of most people today.

The second big block, in my experience, is connected with false expectations about what an information system, particularly one producing a conceptual information output like ESAC's, will do for the user. All too often, a potential user is told that a search on the information system will answer his question or solve his problem. This may be true, or not. It all depends on how he expects to use the output.

Let us assume that his inquiry was properly formulated, a good search strategy was developed, the information base contained some highly relevant material which was pulled, and the search output was well edited. The user then is provided with a set of highly relevant abstracts which speak to his problem area. This does not solve his problem, unless all he wants is a bibliography to adorn his bookshelf. I have been surprised by the number of people who do, in fact, seem to be satisfied in this way.

But the assimilation and application of information requires work, time, and the appropriate training and experience to understand and fit the information in whatever discipline or subject area the problem is concerned with. We have found the most satisfied users of ESAC services to be people, particularly in large industrial organizations or state agencies, who know before they submit an inquiry what the output will look like, and what they will have to do in order to mine the useful information out of the information supplied.

If these blocks to routinely seeking and applying information of the kinds that can be supplied by information and data centers are as serious and widespread as I think they are, perhaps most of us are not so unlike the old Turkish gentleman, after all.

References

(1)   Austen H. Layard, "Discoveries in the Ruins of Nineveh and Babylon." London, 1853, p. 663.

(2)   Jacques Barzun and Henry F. Graff, "The Modern Researcher." New York: Harcourt, Brace & World, 1957, p. 3.

SOCIOECONOMIC ASPECTS OF ENVIRONMENTAL PROBLEMS
SECONDARY INFORMATION SOURCES

James G. Kollegger
President, Environment Information Center, Inc.

Man exercises considerable control over his destiny. Thus, the role of political, economic and other institutions must be considered as interdependent and powerful influences over the future conditions of the world.

—"Environmental Quality, The Third Annual Report of the Council on Environmental Quality," 1972, p. 70 Sup. Doc.

WHAT IS SOCIOECONOMIC INFORMATION?

This question was repeatedly raised during the preparatory sessions for this conference. And since we are about to become involved in systems of socioeconomic information, it is important to understand why this area is of crucial importance. This is essential to my discussion and particularly to understanding the problems one will encounter in dealing with this area of information.

We are fast recognizing that environmental problems must be solved on two planes: the short term (implementing laws, standards and control technology) which is being discussed in the concurrent sessions; and the long term (controlling political, social and economic factors). In other words, a catalytic converter will lessen nitrous oxide pollution from cars, but it doesn't solve the problem of resource consumption, urban sprawl and junkyards. After "The Limits to Growth," "The Blueprint for Survival" and the Stockholm

Conference, we know that pollution is only the tip of the iceberg. Ultimately, all environmental problems stem from five areas.

(1)   Population (growth rates and migration patterns)

(2)   Technology development (including housing, transportation, food production and particularly their energy implications)

(3)   Political dynamics (fiscal, monetary policies, and in particular, governmental standards and incentives)

(4)   Societal behavior and value patterns (the reasons we live, play and work the way we do — environmental behavior)

(5)   Economics (the quantitative relationships between the preceding factors)

A Conceptual Model

Figure 1 is a model which will help conceptualize the relationship among these factors. If we provide some examples, it will help illustrate why an environmental researcher ultimately ends up at the socioeconomic aspects of the problem.

Examples of Socioeconomic Cause-Effect

Example 1: Damming of Wild and Scenic Rivers — Effect: very few western rivers remain in their natural, wild state. Most have been dammed to provide irrigation and drinking water to and generate hydroelectric power. Causes: political pressures emanating from the Southwest. Where excessive migrations in search of cheap land and open space required water for drinking, farming and industry, that was just not there. Meanwhile, however, water-rich land in the South is placed in the land bank and farmers are subsidized to keep land fallow. The root causes: political and economic ones, not just technology.

Example 2: Urban-Suburban Sprawl — Effect: open space is fast disappearing under low density housing developments, shopping centers, parking lots and highways. Causes: the postwar G.I. Bill and the National Defense Highway Act which encouraged single-family home ownership (no down payment) and a highly personalized

Figure 1: Socioeconomic-Environmental Interrelationships — A
Conceptual Model

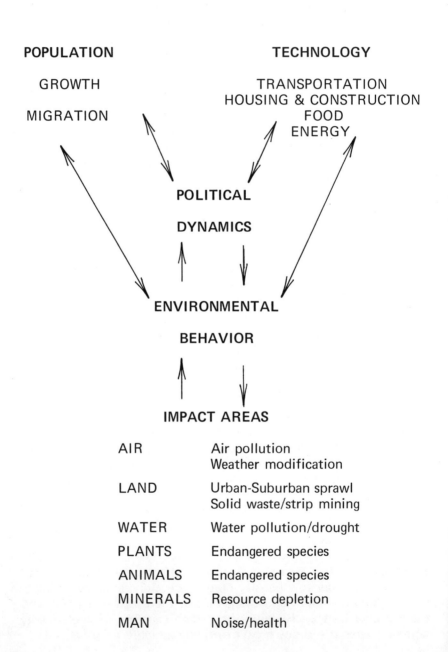

POPULATION   TECHNOLOGY

GROWTH   TRANSPORTATION
                               HOUSING & CONSTRUCTION
MIGRATION   FOOD
                                    ENERGY

POLITICAL

DYNAMICS

ENVIRONMENTAL

BEHAVIOR

IMPACT AREAS

AIR   Air pollution
               Weather modification

LAND   Urban-Suburban sprawl
               Solid waste/strip mining

WATER   Water pollution/drought

PLANTS   Endangered species

ANIMALS   Endangered species

MINERALS   Resource depletion

MAN   Noise/health

transportation mode (the automobile). If we project certain political and economic events occurring today, we can probably project future impact.

Example 3: Federal Auto Emission Standards — Stricter emission standards have resurrected the Wankel engine, a low efficiency, low compression engine that will require lower octane (lead free) fuels, but more of them. What effect will this have on resource consumption?

Example 4: Zero Discharge — If this comes to pass, as it seems likely for certain industries, industrial plants will be freed from waterside locations since all waters can be recycled. There will then be a mass relocation to market areas — cities and suburbs — in order to cut transportation costs. What effect will this have on the transportation industry? On land use? Jobs? If you are an information specialist charged with ferreting out such matters, where do you start?

HORIZONTAL INFORMATION COVERAGE

The Concept of Single Source Access

The rapid emergence of environment as a multidisciplined profession, the resulting information explosion and the infusion of "outsiders" into a hitherto privileged professional sanctuary also created the need for new concepts in information handling. In 1970, when environment was not yet a recognized profession (indeed, when many felt it was a passing public fad), Environment Information Center was created with the express purpose of developing an information system that would closely parallel all aspects of environmental problems — cause and effect. We regarded "environment" as a total, interrelated concept, and built a system that permitted cross-referencing between, for instance, population trends and air pollution. It was conceived as a single-source access sytem which:

(a)   covered all information categories important to environmental problem solving;

(b)   covered all types of media used to convey environmentally significant information: magazines, books, reports, films, conference papers, special publications, speeches;

(c) used all practicable media to disseminate and access information from this data bank, including:

    (1) abstract journals and services,
    (2) annual cumulative subject, industry and author indexes,
    (3) document retrieval services,
    (4) microfiche document subscription and retrieval services,
    (5) computer tape services,
    (6) special searches and studies
    (7) on-line retrieval systems,
    (8) selective dissemination of information.

Both a controlled vocabulary and a conceptual cataloging system were developed for 21 environmental problem areas. This category system permits researchers to enter 21 major cause-effect areas:

Air Pollution	Oceans and Estuaries
Chemical and Biological Contamination	Population Planning and Control Radiological Contamination
Energy	Recreation
Environmental Education	Renewable Resources
Environmental Design	Solid Waste
Food and Drugs	Transportation
General	Water Pollution
International	Weather Modification and Geo-
Land Use and Misuse	physical Change
Noise Pollution	Wildlife
Nonrenewable Resources	

A more detailed description is contained in Appendix B.

Inputs: This system, called Environment Information ACCESS, covers 2,000 international periodicals, government reports and documents, select speeches, research reports, newspaper articles, conference papers and proceedings, books, legislation, Federal Register entries, patents, films.

Throughput: All items are acquired in full document form, abstracted by EIC staff, indexed by subject, industry, author, geography and organization, and often cross-referenced.

Output: The data bank is tapped through a biweekly abstract journal (ACCESS), an annual cumulative index (The Environment Index); hard copy document retrieval (access retrieval), microfiche document retrieval on demand or on a subscription basis per category (Envirofiche); computer tape services (The Environmental Science Citation Index); computer searches (ACCESS Search); and other publications (such as the critical guide, The Environment Film Review).

Other Horizontal Environmental Coverage

ACCESS is unique as a horizontal information system which covers both socioeconomic and environmental impact areas. Some publications do cover more than one area of environmental impact, but these are restricted to the technical aspects of air and water pollution. The best example is Pollution Abstracts, issued six times per year, which covers seven contamination areas. Pollution Abstracts provides cumulated indexes, and document retrieval, air, fresh water, marine, land, noise, sewage, and general. A publication called Environmental Periodicals covers similar areas by providing the contents pages of journals. It too offers document retrieval.

General Horizontal Information Sources

These range in sophistication from simple citation listings, such as the Wilson Reader's Guide, which covers a relatively small sample of total journal literature, to ISI'S Current Contents, which covers 3,500. The Science Citation Index, for instance, is a system which permits one to locate articles based on the type of references they quote; offers profiling, SDI and tearsheet retrieval.

SECONDARY INFORMATION SOURCES — VERTICAL COVERAGE

Few secondary information sources deal with socioeconomic matters in a vertical sense. Someone researching population, for instance, is not nearly as well served as someone researching water pollution. Aside from environmental coverage offered by ACCESS, such areas as housing, transportation, population, etc. are not extensively served by their own abstract, index, retrieval and search services.

For purposes of this discussion, the word "vertical" refers to the five major areas in the Model I discussed earlier.

(1) Population
(2) Technology Development (including transport,
      housing, food)
(3) Political Dynamics
(4) Societal Behavior and Values (including recreation)
(5) Economics: the quantitative relationships among
      all these

A list of sources follows in Appendix A. Emphasis here is on bibliographic systems rather than hard data, since the bibliographic ultimately leads to hard data; but a select scattering of important hard
data sources — such as the Census — is also included. Let me briefly
summarize the five areas.

Population

Most hard data comes from the Bureau of the Census, or the United
Nations (UNESCO). Not only does the Census measure the crucial
inputs of population growth and migration, it also provides data applicable to housing, employment, business statistics, education and
recreation. Much of it will probably go into the new SUMSTAT
(Summary statistics) program now being conceptualized. Until then,
however, the best way to unearth Census data is through the quarterly Bureau of the Census Catalog, which also announces tape services, or through the monthly Catalog of Government Publications.
Bibliographic information on population control is best obtained
through ACCESS (abstracts) or the Population Index (citations only).

Technology

According to Barry Commoner, this is where it's at, but it is very
hard to get at. (That is, monitor new technologies and their potential impacts.) Aside from the horizontal coverage of ACCESS, one
must consult several dozen sources: the Census, departments of Transportation, Housing, Commerce (Patent Office) and trade associations,
and such commercial services as F.W. Dodge Corp. (a division of
McGraw-Hill) which measures housing starts, new permits, etc.; or
Engineering Index, a monthly abstract service.

Political

My earlier examples illustrated how potent Federal laws, standards
and incentives can be. To keep up with new legislation, agency
decisions and Federal programs, the various legal services (which are

being covered in a concurrent session) are probably best. Congressional Information Service is a good way to follow the workings of Congress; but probably the best way to get a qualitative feel for what's going on is through primary media (National Journal, New York Times, Congressional Quarterly). All of these have companion indexes.

Societal Behavior and Values

I am really speaking of an emerging field called "environmental behavior" — why and how man works, creates, plays, the means of housing and transportation he chooses (rather than the actual technology). Aside from raw statistics provided by the Census and Bureau of Outdoor Recreation(Recreation Register), coverage is restricted to primary publications such as Sage publications journal Environment and Behavior and RC's Design and Environment. The journal literature is best followed through ACCESS or Current Contents.

Economics

A wealth of raw data is available from Federal agencies and commercial services. Every conceivable quantitative aspect seems to be catalogued: power consumption, distribution patterns, resource depletion, employment. Useful secondary sources include Predicasts, which cross-references statistics with bibliographic sources. Example: tons of coal consumed in the U.S. is contrasted with baseline data; source of data is given; and data can be retrieved by subject or Standard Industrial Classifications.

Two excellent sources that should not be overlooked are: CEQ whose Annual Report is an encyclopedia of sociotechnoeconomic facts; and the Council on Economic Priorities, a nonprofit public interest group which issues well-documented studies on the social and environmental impacts of economic behavior. Names, addresses, products and prices of these services follow.

We opened this discussion with a question: why socioeconomic information? I'd like to close with an answer — a quote taken from the CEQ Annual Report:

"Man is not a captive of uncontrollable forces. He can exercise a significant degree of control over his future if he has some idea of the problems which lie ahead."

Hopefully this presentation has contributed to a better understanding of how this can be done.

APPENDIX A — SELECT ROSTER OF SECONDARY INFORMATION SOURCES

Population Dynamics

Primary Source Data:

> Bureau of Census (U.S.)
> Publications Distribution Section
> Washington, D.C. 20233

>> Current Population Reports ($14.00)
>> (includes 8 series of reports, e.g., "Population Characteristics," "Population Estimates and Projections. Monthly Estimates of the Total Population of the U.S." - monthly, "Farm Population," etc.)

> Statistical Office of the United Nations
> Department of Economic and Social Affairs
> United Nations
> New York, New York 10017

>> Population and Vital Statistics Report
>> (quarterly update on population and vital statistics for every country of the world; $4.00)

Secondary/Bibliographic Sources:

> Office of Population Research
> Princeton University
> 5 Ivy Lane
> Princeton, New Jersey 08540

>> Population Index (Q, $15.00)

> Environment Information Center, Inc.
> 124 East 39th Street
> New York, New York 10016

>> Environment Information ACCESS
>> (SM, $150.00) Category 13

Health Services and Mental Health Administration
Department of Health, Education, and Welfare
5600 Fishers Lane, Room 12A-33
Rockville, Maryland 20852

Family Planning Digest (BM)

Population Council
245 Park Avenue
New York, New York 10017

Current Publications in Population/Family
    Planning (M)

Reproduction Research Information Service Ltd.
141 Newmarket Road
Cambridge, England

Bibliography of Reproduction (M)

Technology Development — Transportation

Primary Source Data:

Bureau of Census (U.S.)
Chief of the Transportation Division
Washington, D.C. 20233

1967 Census of Transportation

(a) Commodity Transportation Survey, 1967:

Shipments from Production Area to Destination Area (contains 484,000 records,
available on four reels of computer tape,
either IBM/360 7- or 9-track, or Univac
1107, 9-track)

(b) Commodity Transportation Survey, 1967:

Shipments from State of Origin to State
of Destination (contains 705,000 records,
available on five reels of tape, either
IBM/360 7- or 9-track, or Univac 1107,
9-track)

Secondary/Bibliographic Sources:

Environment Information Center, Inc.
124 East 39th Street
New York, New York 10016

Environment Information ACCESS (SM, $150.00)
Category 18 Transportation

Society of Automotive Engineers (SAE)
Two Pennsylvania Plaza
New York, New York 10001

SAE Publications/Readers Service
(papers and technical information developed
by SAE, cited in SAE Journal of Automotive
Engineering, M)

Northwestern University Transportation Center
1818 Hinman Avenue
Evanston, Illinois 60204

Current Literature in Traffic and Transportation
(M, $6.00)

Highway Research Board
National Academy of Sciences
2101 Constitution Avenue
Washington, D.C. 20418

Highway Research Abstracts (M, $5.00)
Highway Research Information Service Abstracts
(Q, $20.00) (abstracts of actual research
in progress)

U.S. Department of Transportation (DOT)
Washington, D.C. 20590

United Engineering Library
395 East 47th Street
New York, New York 10017

Engineering Index (M)
Compendex

Institute for Scientific Information
325 Chestnut Street
Philadelphia, Pa. 19105

> Current Contents: Engineering & Technology (W, $100)

H.W. Wilson
950 University Avenue
Bronx, New York 10452

> Applied Science & Technology Index (M, price varies)

Technology Development — Housing

Primary Source Data:

Bureau of Census
Publication Distribution Section
Washington, D.C. 20233

> General Housing Characteristics (1970 statistics;
>   58 reports, $61.35)
> Current Housing Reports: Housing Vacancies
>   (Q and A, $1.50)

McGraw-Hill Information Systems
F.W. Dodge Co.
1221 Avenue of the Americas
New York, New York

> Dodge Reports

Secondary/Bibliographic Sources:

Environment Information Center, Inc.
124 East 39th Street
New York, New York 10016

> Environment Information ACCESS (SM, $150.00)
>   Category 05 Environmental Design

U.S. Department of Housing and Urban Development (HUD)
Washington, D.C. 20410

> Housing and Urban Development Trends (M)

Housing and Renewal Services
1319 F Street N.W.
Washington, D.C. 20004

Housing and Renewal Index (SM, $60.00)

National Association of Home Builders of the U.S. (NAHB)
1625 L Street N.W.
Washington, D.C. 20036

Library Bulletin (M, free to members)

Technology Development — Energy

Primary Source Data:

Federal Power Commission
Office of Public Information
Washington, D.C. 20426

FPC News (W, free)
Federal Power Statistics

Secondary/Bibliographic Sources:

Environment Information Center, Inc.
124 East 39th Street
New York, New York 10016

Environment Information ACCESS (SM, $150.00)
Category 03 Energy

Institute for Scientific Information
325 Chestnut Street
Philadelphia, Pa. 19106

Current Contents (W, $100 per service)
Science Citation Index
OATS (tearsheet service)
ASCA (profile searches)

Technology Development — Resource Use

Primary Source Data:

Bureau of Census
Washington, D.C. 20233

1967 Census of Mineral Industries (14 reports, $8.10)
Area Statistics (49 reports, $16.80)

Secondary/Bibliographic Sources:

Environment Information Center, Inc.
124 East 39th Street
New York, New York 10016

Environment Information ACCESS (SM, $150.00)
Categories 11 Nonrenewable Resources
Categories 15 Terrestrial Resources
Categories 16 Water Resources

American Petroleum Institute
555 Madison Avenue
New York, New York 10022

Abstracts of Air and Water Conservation Literature
and Patents (W, $275-550)
Abstracts of Petroleum Substitutes Literature and
Patents (M, $150-275)
Abstracts of Refining Literature (W, $1,100-13,000)
Abstracts of Refining Patents (W, $2,000-10,000)
Abstracts of Transportation and Storage Literature
and Patents (M, $275-550)

Institute for Scientific Information
325 Chestnut Street
Philadelphia, Pa. 19106

Current Contents:
Engineering & Technology (W, $100)
Physical & Chemical Science (W, $100)
Life Sciences (W, $100)

H.W. Wilson Co.
950 University Avenue
Bronx, New York 10452

Biological and Agricultural Index (M, price varies)

Technology Development — Food

Primary Source Data:

Food and Agriculture Organization of the U.N. (FAO)
Documentation Centre
Via delle Terme di Caracalla
Rome, Italy

FAO Documentation - Current Index (M, free)

Secondary/Bibliographic Data:

Environment Information Center, Inc.
124 East 39th Street
New York, New York 10016

Environment Information ACCESS (SM, $150.00)
Category of Food & Drugs

Institute for Scientific Information
325 Chestnut Street
Philadelphia, Pa. 19106

Current Contents:
Agricultural, Food & Vet. Sciences (W, $100)

General Product Information:

Thomas Publishing Co.
461 8th Avenue
New York, New York

Thomas Register (catalog service)

United States Patent Office
Washington, D.C. 20231

Official Gazette (W, $78.00)

Political Dynamics

Bibliographic Sources:

Environment Information Center
124 East 39th Street
New York, New York 10016

Environment Information ACCESS (SM, $150)
Categories 1-21; 07 General, 08 International

Bureau of National Affairs (BNA)
1231 25th Street
Washington, D.C. 20037

Environment Reporter (M, $100)

New York Times Company
229 West 43rd Street
New York, New York 10036

New York Times Index (SM, $78; microfilm
$525-3,035)
New York Times Data Bank (an on-line retrieval
system now under development)

Commerce Clearinghouse, Inc. (CCH)
4025 W. Peterson Avenue
Chicago, Illinois

Various legal documentation services.

Congressional Information Service
500 Montgomery Building
Washington, D.C. 20014

CIS Index (M, price varies $95-395)
Annual Index ($190)

H.W. Wilson Co.
950 University Avenue
Bronx, New York 10452

Index to Legal Periodicals (M, price varies)

Societal Behavior (Environmental Behavior)

Primary Source Data:

Bureau of Labor Statistics
U.S. Department of Labor
14th Street and Constitution Avenue
Washington, D.C. 20210

Monthly Labor Review ($9.00)

League of Federal Recreation Assn. Inc.
927 15th Street N.W.
Washington, D.C. 20005

Recreation Register (M)

Bureau of Outdoor Recreation
U.S. Department of the Interior
Washington, D.C. 20240

Selected Outdoor Recreation Statistics
(March 1971, 145 p., $1.25)

Secondary/Bibliographic Sources:

Sociological Abstracts
73 8th Avenue
Brooklyn, New York 11215

Sociological Abstracts (8/year, $100; cum. index
every 10 years) (divided into 28 areas of
sociology; provides hard copy retrieval of
articles and conference papers)

H.W. Wilson Co.
950 University Avenue
Bronx, New York 10452

Social Sciences and Humanities Index
(M, price varies)

Economics

Primary Source Data:

Dun & Bradstreet
99 Church Street
New York, New York 10007

DMI - Dun Market Identifiers — lists 3 million
businesses, providing: sales volume, number of
employees, net worth, when started.
Cost: $40-155 per M.

McGraw-Hill Information Systems
F.W. Dodge Divison
New York, New York

Dodge Reports — compilation of all new construction projects in a given area on a daily basis;
lists location, contractor data, bidding information;
price varies.

Standard & Poors
345 Hudson Street
New York, New York

Compustat — machine readable tape service providing historical financial information on large
companies 20 years back. Price varies, but complete package is $25,000.

ISL Tapes (Investment Statistics) — daily stock
transactions, corporate pricing, bond pricing,
$750-9,000.

Chase Econometrics, Inc.
555 City Line Avenue
Bala-Cynwyd, Pa. 19004

Various reports, economic data bases, macro-
economic models, industry models, economic
consulting.

Interactive Data Corp.
486 Totten Pond Road
Waltham, Mass. 02154

On-line terminals: national income and product
accounts, GNP & Components by Industry, new
management and equipment expenditures, retail
and wholesale trade and inventory.

Secondary/Bibliographic Sources:

Predicasts, Inc.
10550 Park Lane
University Circle
Cleveland, Ohio 44106

Funk and Scott Index of Corporations and
Industries (W, $132) — covers analysis, opinions,
forecasts and newsworthy items appearing in trade
and financial press, analytical reports of investment
services, bank newsletters; covers articles by industry,
product and subject; also by S.I.C. codes.

Predicasts (Q, $172) — economic and forecast
statistics, consists of summary forecasts with historical data from 1957-68; composite forecasts for
1969, 1970, 1975 and 1980 on general economics,
products, transportation, construction, capital index spending, key world forecasts and capacity
forecasts; also general economic abstracts on population, labor force and employment, national income and expenditure, production and business
capacity, construction and source of forecasts.

Environment Information Center, Inc.
124 East 39th Street
New York, New York 10016

Environment Information ACCESS (SM, $150)

Compendium Publishers International Corp.
2175 Lemoine Avenue
Fort Lee, New Jersey 07024

> SEARCH: 19 divisions (M, $25-60)
> chemical, production data

Council on Environmental Quality
722 Jackson Place, N.W.
Washington, D.C. 20006

> Annual Report (Environmental Quality)
> third report, 1972

Council on Economic Priorities
456 Greenwich Street
New York, New York 10013

> Economic Priorities Report (BM, $20)
> also in-depth studies on electric power
> and utility and paper industries

H.W. Wilson Co.
950 University Avenue
Bronx, New York 10452

> Business Periodicals Index (M, price varies)

APPENDIX B — ACCESS CLASSIFICATION SYSTEM

(1) Air Pollution: Includes air pollution aspects of aircraft and auto emissions, emissions from extracting, refining and manufacturing industries, incineration, electric power generation, industrial and residential heating, airborne gases, particulates, thermal air pollution.

(2) Chemical and Biological Contamination: Includes contamination aspects of chemicals and biological agents — chemical and biological warfare, plant and animal diseases, pests; agricultural chemicals — pesticides, fungicides, herbicides, insecticides, fertilizers; metal poisoning — mercury lead, zinc; detergents — phosphates, nitrates.

(3) Energy: Includes energy aspects of nuclear and conventional electric power generation, fission, fusion, hydroelectric, pumped storage, chemical, unconventional — solar, geothermal, waves and tides.

(4) Environmental Education: Includes both philosophical and operational aspects; curriculum planning and development; environmental study areas as a subject and academic discipline, including adult and community educational programs.

(5) Environmental Design and Urban Ecology: Includes building and landscape architecture and esthetic aspects of nonbuilding architecture; visual pollution — signs, billboards, transmission lines.

(6) Food and Drugs: Includes impact of environmental problems on food — agriculture, commercial fisheries, dairy farming, ranching; food processing and canning; harvest expansion and miracle crops, nutritional requirements; food poisoning and contamination.

(7) General: Includes general policy, planning and programs by Federal, state and local governments, industrial trade associations, corporations, pollution control industries, environmental organizations, legal and political aspects; environmental education; problem solving, systems analysis and computer applications. For specific pollution abatement programs, see individual categories.

(8) International: Includes international and non-U.S. environmental issues; pollution and conservation problems, international cooperation, United Nations and other world agency programs.

(9) Land Use and Misuse: Includes use and abuse of land and

wetlands — land reclamation, power and pipeline transmission, sub-divisons, construction, stripmining; planning — scenic and historic preservation, open space, urban and regional planning; recreational and real estate uses of land, including camping and wilderness.

(10) Noise Pollution: Includes sources and effects of noise from air-craft, vehicles, railroads and rapid transit, construction, explosives, electronics; physiological and psychological effects.

(11) Nonrenewable Resources: Includes resource aspects of minerals and fossil fuels (coal, petroleum, natural gas).

(12) Oceans and Estuaries: Includes use and abuse of ocean environment; international agreements on seabed use, technology and programs for exploitation — ocean mining, farming, off-shore activities; oceanography.

(13) Population Planning and Control: Includes physical, psychological and socioeconomic aspects of population growth, incentives and regulations, birth control techniques — fertility adjustment, contraception, abortion, sterilization; death control.

(14) Radiological Contamination: Includes sources and effects of atomic and electromagnetic radiation — mine accidents, mine tailings, seepage, waste disposal, fallout, lab accidents, reactor accidents; x-rays, extra-terrestrial and microwave radiation, physiological and psychological effects.

(15) Renewable Resources — Terrestrial: Includes renewal aspects of plants and soil (for animals and animal habitat, see category 21); forest management, tree farms, reforestation, new strains, logging; soil conservation; botany (for land use and abuse, see category 9).

(16) Renewable Resources — Water: Includes renewal aspects of water (for pollution aspects, see category 19); water tables, water-sheds, water resources, irrigation, flood control, man-made lakes, channelization, water purification, desalination, water supply; limnology (for ocean and marine resources, see category 12).

(17) Solid Waste: Includes refuse collection and disposal — litter and municipal refuse; sanitary landfill and waste structures, compaction and pulverization, incineration, water burial; waste reduction — package redesign, recycling and reuse (cryogenic reduction, plasma torch, destructive distillation).

(18) Transportation: Includes transportation aspects of motor vehicles and highways, aircraft and airports, railroads, ships, mass transit; pipeline transportation; new systems and concepts; safety.

(19) Water Pollution: Includes water pollution aspects of industrial, municipal, and agricultural effluents, thermal, oil, chemical, fertilizer and phosphate eutrophication, animal wastes; municipal sewage and detergents, dyes, treatment systems and processes; limnology, hydrospheric sciences.

(20) Weather Modification and Geophysical Change: Includes geophysical impact of use and misuse of environmental resources; unintentional and deliberate weather modification, climate control; effects of carbon dioxide and particle accumulation, vapor trails, reflective effects of oil slicks, thermal pockets (cities); monitoring and sensing techniques, meteorology and atmospheric sciences.

(21) Wildlife: Includes fish and wildlife, game preserves, wildlife management, bird sanctuaries, endangered and vanishing species, animal habitat, ichthyology and zoology.

SELECTED LISTING OF
INFORMATION CENTERS AND SERVICES
AVAILABLE IN THE SOCIOECONOMIC AREA

A large number of public and private organizations and agencies have been created during the past decade that focus on various facets of the socioeconomic aspects of the environment. Publications listing such centers and services have been released and continue to be updated as organizations and agencies are created, expanded, modified or deleted.

Two relatively comprehensive publications found to be extremely useful by users queried for our presentation are the following:

Encyclopedia of Information Systems and Services, 1971, edited by Anthony T. Kruzas and available from:

> Academic Media
> 32 Lincoln Avenue
> Orange, New Jersey 07050
>
> Price: $67.50

This publication provides descriptions of over 800 organizations in the United States and Canada. Information includes computer systems; information centers; data bases and services; library and information networks; data banks; documentation centers; literature storage and retrieval systems; micrographic services; research centers; clearinghouses and referral centers; and others. Subject, institution and personnel indexes provided are also useful. Like any publication of this type, some of the information provided is dated.

Directory of Consumer Protection and Environmental
Agencies, compiled by the California Center for
Public Affairs and available from:

Academic Media
32 Lincoln Avenue
Orange, New Jersey 07050

Price: $39.50

This directory is national in scope and includes descriptive information of national, regional, state and selected government and private organizations concerned with the quality of the natural and physical environment. Particular emphasis is given to those involved in formulating or influencing policy, regulation, control management, education and information.

In the process of reviewing available information sources and services, we have selected and described a number of organizations and services that are established and that cover a range of types of services and aspects of socioeconomic data.

INFORMATION CENTERS AND SERVICES

Housing and Urban Development Library
Department of Housing and Urban
     Development
7th and D Street, S.W.
Washington, D.C. 20410

Tel. (202) 755-6376

Mrs. Elsa S. Freeman directs a staff of approximately 40 persons, more than half of whom are professionals. The Library provides the usual library services: references, inter-library loan, information searches. A program information center distributes HUD publications. The Library receives its information on American and foreign housing and community developments from Federal, state and local agencies, commercial sources and printed and nonpublished materials. Holdings include approximately 455,000 volumes. The Library's facilities are available to the public for in-house use. There is no charge for most services. Bibliographies are sold by the Government Printing Office and the National Technical Information Service.

National Planning Association
1606 New Hampshire Avenue, N.W.
Washington, D.C. 20009

Tel. (202) 265-7685

Michael E. Carbine is the Information Director for the Association
which has a staff of 100 persons, 60 to 70% of whom are professionals. The Association publishes Looking Ahead ten times a year,
various pamphlets, policy statements and special reports on an irregular basis, Projection Highlights eight times per year, and the
National and Regional Economic Projections Series annually.

The Association performs technical research work and the results
are disseminated to its members and subscribers through its various
publications. Special research projects will be undertaken on a contract basis. The scope of the Association's concern includes domestic and international economic planning and cooperation and policy
issue. Information bases are agriculture, business, labor and the professions. Holdings number about 80,000 volumes. Typical users of
NPA materials are market researchers, contractors and government
agencies.

NPA is expanding its work in environmental planning and research
under Mr. Ivars Gutmanis, who will be a speaker at the EPA symposium.

Smithsonian Science Information
    Exchange
1730 M Street, N.W.
Washington, D.C. 20036

Tel. (202) 381-5511

The Smithsonian Science Information Exchange, Inc. is headed by
Dr. David F. Hersey, President. The Exchange collects 85,000 to
100,000 single page records of ongoing research projects each year.
Contributed projects may be funded by public or private sources.
Each record describes who supports the project, who does it, where
and when the research is performed, and usually includes a technical
summary of the project. Basic and applied research in life, physical
social, behavioral and engineering sciences is covered.

Information is available in areas as specific or general as the requester desires. Subject searches, administrative information searches, standard tabulations of current projects and historical searches will be performed for varying fee schedules. Write for the latest price list. Requests for services are accepted by phone or mail. Information is usually in the mail within ten days.

National Technical Information Service
United States Department of Commerce
5285 Port Royal Road
Springfield, Virginia 22151

Tel. (703) 321-8888

William T. Knox is the Director of the National Technical Information Service, which employs over 300 persons including administrative officers, reference and information specialists, researchers and publishing and photocopying personnel. Reports and tape files of data from Federal agencies and their contractors are catalogued, abstracted and indexed. A semimonthly abstract journal as well as numerous special subject bulletins are published to apprise users of the documents available. Publications and reports are sold to the public in paper form or microfiche. Special catalogs, journals and bibliographies are also produced. Information searches are performed on request.

The subject matter covered by NTIS documents includes research, engineering, study and analysis and technical reports. The Service handles in excess of 50,000 documents each year. The entire collection exceeds 680,000 titles, 100,000 of which are currently in stock. Anyone may use NTIS. Price lists are available on request.

Division of Information Services
Bureau of Labor Statistics
Department of Labor
441 G Street, N.W.
Washington, D.C. 20212

Tel. (202) 961-2913

Chief of the Divison of Information Services is Kathryn D. Hoyle. A staff of two economists, seven nonprofessional information specialists and eight clerical personnel collect labor statistics including information on the labor force, employment and unemployment, collective bargaining, wage scales, wholesale and consumer prices, injury statistics and economic projection. Information is received from workers, businessmen, other Government agencies, all of whom contribute voluntarily, the Census Bureau and surveys conducted by BLS field staff. The Division maintains an extensive collection of bulletins, reports and periodicals. Information is disseminated in special bulletins and the Monthly Labor Review.

Specific information requests may be phoned in or written. A walk-in information office is located in Room 1539 of the General Accounting Building at 441 G Street, N.W., Washington D.C., and at various field offices. There are no restrictions on who may use the Division's servcies, most of which are provided free of charge.

The Urban Institute Library
2100 M Street, N.W.
Washington, D.C. 20037

Tel. (202) 223-1950

A staff of four information and library professionals, including the Director, Judy Fair, and five clerical and nonprofessional personnel collect and organize information dealing with urban matters. They provide consulting, copying, interlibrary loan, manual literature searches, reference and referral services, selected dissemination of information services, state-of-the-art compilations and microreproduction services.

Urban Institute is published 50 to 60 times a year and is composed primarily of working papers, reports and monographs. The Library's 10,000 holdings include 7,000 reports and 3,000 books. Information is gathered from Urban Affairs Abstracts, The National League of Cities, universities, Governmental agencies and voluntary contributions as well as usual library resources.

The staff members will answer specific inquiries from the District of Columbia area, but their services are generally restricted to Urban Institute researchers. Services are not available to the general public. They are not equipped to handle outside inquiries now.

National Clearinghouse for Drug
Abuse Information
Department of Health, Education
and Welfare
5600 Fishers Lane
Rockville, Maryland 20852

Tel. (202) 443-4443

Mrs. Jean McMillan is the Acting Director of the Clearinghouse.
Seven information specialists, five information handlers, six clerical
personnel and six data processing personnel collect and disseminate
published information and NIMH brochures. Specific questions are
answered by information specialists who send out reprints of published articles, lists, indexes and abstracts of pertinent published
articles. The staff makes no attempt to evaluate the materials used.

Any question having to do with drug abuse is within the scope of
Clearinghouse's competence. Their holdings consist of 10,000 articles
and documents and books and 2,000 programs derived from various
sources. The literature is abstracted under a private contract. There
are no restrictions on use of the service. Single publications are provided free as long as they are in stock; multiple copies must be purchased from the Government Printing Office or from the original
source at charge. Typical users are educators, students and the general public. Call or write for general or specific information.

Information Services Office
(Southeast Michigan Council
of Governments)
American Institute of Planners
8th Floor, Book Building
1249 Washington Boulevard
Detroit, Michigan 48226

Tel. (313) 961-4266

Jim Thomas is the Information Services Officer. A staff of two
professionals and ten clerical personnel handle information inquiries
within the scope of planning: legislation, metropolitan development,
advocate planning, national urban policy, urban affairs, education,
transportation, state planning, Federal programs, pollution, AIP
chapters, land use, public facilities and natural resources. Their body

of knowledge includes scientific reports, privately published materials generated in the Southeast Michigan area, the entire resources of the former Transportation and Land Use Study and the Regional Planning Commission, as well as documents from the State of Michigan and local area governments.

Publications include the AIP Journal and the AIP Newsletter. There are various subscription costs. In some cases, member costs are discounted. Reproduction of documents are provided at photocopy cost. Inquiries may be phoned or written.

New County, USA Center
National Association of Counties
1001 Connecticut Avenue, N.W.
Washington, D.C. 20036

Tel. (202) 628-4701

Rodney L. Kendig is the Director of New County, USA Center, which comprises the NACO Living Library. A staff of four professionals and two nonprofessionals utilize the approximately 300 documents of the Living Library and daily contacts with county officials and other public interest groups, research and citizen organizations and academia, as well as the Center's extensive files on county improvement and modernization programs, which handles inquiries from county officials, planners, student and citizen groups concerning ongoing and completed county improvement programs. The Center provides research documents, technical assistance to counties, and on-site consultation services to its subscribing counties. Key studies on county environmental achievements can be obtained from the Living Library at duplication cost.

National League of Cities/U.S. Con-
        ference of Mayors
Library Reference and Inquiry Service
1612 K Street, N.W.
Washington, D.C. 20036

Tel. (202) 293-7375

A staff of fifteen, including six professionals, is headed by William Smith and operates a reference and inquiry service along with the regular services provided by the NLC/USCOM Library. Staff members will answer questions on any aspect of municipal affairs. City and State legislation, government and administration, citizen participation, community development, education, environmental quality, health, housing, intergovernmental relations, manpower, public safety, revenue and finance, transportation and international municipal cooperation are recognized categories of knowledge in which the service maintains current information about ongoing and completed projects and studies.

The Library contains over 30,000 books and reports, 800 periodicals and various municipal codes and city reports, Census data, State Leagues of Cities reports and biographies of selected mayors. The holdings are gathered from typical library sources as well as from the Federal Government, local governments and public interest groups.

The Library publishes an index to Municipal League publications monthly and abstracts the articles from its 800 periodicals weekly in Urban Affairs Abstracts. The inquiry responses are documented and references are provided for further or more indepth information.

The Library and Reference Service is designed to meet the needs of city government researchers and officials, but the staff members will answer inquiries from Federal Government agencies, school districts, civic groups and some private individual requests as their time and work load permit. Typical users are staff of the National League of Cities/U.S. Conference of Mayors, state leagues of cities, city officials, civic groups, Federal agencies and state governments. Requests may be phoned or written.

> Management Information Service
> International City Management Association
> 1140 Connecticut Avenue, N.W.
> Washington, D.C. 20036
>
> Tel. (202) 293-2200

The Management Information Service, headed by Walter Webb, accumulates files from city documents, operations, personnel and budget manuals and utilizes ICMA library facilities, as well as contacts with member cities and other professional management organizations to answer inquiries on any management oriented problem from its subscribers and contract purchasers. Its holdings of city documents approximates 10,000 reports. While there are three full-time professionals handling such inquiries, the full resources and expertise of the International City Management Association are at their disposal.

Users are restricted to subscribers to MIS and private research organizations and universities which have purchased services under contract. Subscription fees are based on the size of a city's population. Requests for information may be phoned in or written and an acknowledgment estimating the length of time required for a full response will be sent within 48 hours.

> Urban Technology Clearinghouse
> Public Technology, Incorporated
> 1140 Connecticut Avenue, N.W.
> Washington, D.C. 20036
>
> Tel. (202) 833-9484

C. Nelson Hay is in charge of the design of a clearinghouse operation to apply technological advancements and improvements to the needs of state and local governments. The Clearinghouse will define and describe the problems to be addressed and will interface with industrial, governmental and institutional resources for solutions. Plans for the program to become operational are tentatively set for Spring, 1973.

> American Institutes for Research (AIR)
> Center for Research in Social Systems (CRESS)
> 10605 Concord Street
> Kensington, Maryland 20795
>
> Tel. (301) 933-3115

Mr. Preston S. Abbott is the Director of this center which has a staff of approximately 25 information and library professional; 35 clerical and nonprofessional. Areas covered include social and behavioral sciences such as area studies, urban problems, and interdisciplinary research. Monographs, journal articles and government technical reports are abstracted by professional staff and indexed according to CRESS-developed Thesaurus of Social Science Index Terms. Bibliographic and analysis services are available on a fee basis according to specifically framed request; other services available by appointment only.

American Medical Association (AMA)
Archive-Library
535 North Dearborn Street
Chicago, Illinois 60610

Tel. (312) 527-1500
TWX 910-221-1300

Dr. Susan Crawford is the Director of the Archive-Library. The Archive-Library is concerned with medicine, including the history of medicine, organized medicine, and sociological and economic aspects of medicine. Data are obtained on a continuous basis from published literature and internally generated documents. Holdings are extensive and include books, articles and nonprint materials.

Services include the following: data collection and analysis; depository; interlibrary loan; manual literature searching; reference and referral services; research; SDI services; state-of-the-art compilation. Medical Socioeconomic Research Resources is also available on a subscription basis.

Ecology Forum, Inc.
Environment Information Center (EIC)
124 East 39th Street
New York, New York 10016

Tel. (212) 685-0845

Mr. James G. Kollegger is President of EIC, Inc. The Environment Information Center (EIC) is a computer-assisted central data bank which gathers, indexes, abstracts, analyzes and disseminates information on environmental matters. EIC monitors abstracts and cross-references information appearing in a large number of scientific, trade and general periodicals. EIC makes this information available to subscribers in publication form (Environment Information ACCESS) or through computer searches and bibliography assemblies requested by mail or telephone order. Environmental issues covered include air, noise, land pollution; wildlife's geophysical change; energy; recreation; transportation; population control; ecological imbalance.

Environment Information ACCESS includes descriptions of books, periodicals, conferences, legislation; special focus on one subject in each issue; available by yearly subscription. Various other reports are issued on an irregular basis. Many items appearing in ACCESS are available in microfiche or hard copy form on a single item or a subscription basis. Assistance can be given in locating special items, assembling data or bibliographies, and obtaining literature surveys and summaries.

> Joint Council on Economic Education (JCEE)
> 1212 Avenue of the Americas
> New York, New York 10036
>
> Tel. (212) 582-5150

Dr. M.L. Frankel is President of JCEE. JCEE serves as a clearinghouse for ideas, people, programs and material that can effect economic understanding. It provides newsletters to various audiences and is available to help with any economic education program or suggest new efforts. Publications include Journal of Economic Education and several newsletters. Publications are intended for several levels: elementary, junior high, senior high and college. General bibliographies and films are provided. Workshops are sponsored.

> National Council on Crime and Delinquency
> Information Center on Crime and Delinquency (ICCD)
> 345 Park Avenue
> New York, New York 10022
>
> Tel. (212) 254-7110.

Mr. Eugene Doleschal is Acting Director of ICCD. Information Center on Crime and Delinquency (ICCD) maintains the world's largest library on crime and delinquency. The Center compiles bibliographic references and abstracts with emphasis on research and on innovative and promising programs and proposals. In addition to abstracting and information processing, the staff evaluates, synthesizes and disseminates information on given topics. Scope of coverage is concerned with prevention, control and treatment of crime and juvenile delinquency. Over 100 journals, 2,000 books, pamphlets, government documents, and fugitive literature are reviewed annually. A quarterly publication, Crime and Delinquency

<u>Literature</u>, is available by yearly subscription. Literature searches
and state-of-the-art compilations are done by the staff.

New York Times Company
Information Bank
229 West 43rd Street
New York, New York 10036

Tel. (212) 556-1234

Dr. John Rothman is the Director, Library and Information Services.
The New York Times Information Bank serves as a centralized computer facility for the input, storage and retrieval of information from
The New York Times and other publications. Covered are political,
economic and social affairs from The New York Times and selected
material from over 70 other publications. Holdings include the existing clipping library of The New York Times from the last fifty years
in selected subjects; the total file comprises some 20 million clippings
files under some 80,000 subject classifications and about 1,250,000
names. The New York Times Index is produced from the information bank.

Demand bibliographies from data base can be requested. Source
material are stored on microfiche produced by Microfilming Corporation of America, a subsidiary of The New York Times. Microfiche are available on request. Computer searches, reference service and SDI service are also available.

U.S. Bureau of the Census
Public Information Office
Room 2089, Building 3
Washington, D.C. 20233

Tel. (301) 763-7273

Mr. William Lerner is Chief of Data User Services Division. The
Public Information Office coordinates and provides technical data
and services to divisons of the U.S. Bureau of the Census and other
agencies. It supports the Census Bureau as a general purpose statistical agency and collects, tabulates and publishes a wide variety of
data about the people and the economy of the United States.
Weekly, monthly, quarterly, semiannual and annual publications

are available. Microfiche of most reports issued since January 1, 1968 is available in 4 x 6 inch format; 16 mm. microfilm of selected items is also available. Several categories of items are available on magnetic tape. Coding guides and geographic base files are available for most metropolitan areas.

University Microfilms
Direct Access to Reference Infor-
     mation (DATRIX)
300 North Zeeb Road
Ann Arbor, Michigan 48106

Tel. (313) 761-4700

Mr. Richard T. Wood is Group Product Manager. Direct Access to Reference Information (DATRIX) is a computerized information retrieval system employed to manipulate the file of dissertation references at University Microfilms. This file consists of approximately 185,000 references from some 250 volumes of Dissertation Abstracts dating from 1938. All doctoral dissertations listed in Dissertation Abstracts from 1938 to date, including 77 major subject and 119 minor subject areas, are included. The program has recently been broadened to include some foreign universities in addition to the participating universities in the United States and Canada.

Copies of the complete dissertations listed in the DATRIX base are available on 35 mm. microfilm roll or as xerographic hard copy. Services are available on a fee basis; keyword lists are available for guidance in preparing an order.

University of North Carolina
Institute for Research in Social Science
Social Science Data Center
Manning Hall, Room 10
Chapel Hill, North Carolina 27514

Tel. (919) 933-1174 Extension 28

Mr. Richard Rockwell is Director of Social Science Data Library. The center maintains survey data in political science, anthropology, social welfare, sociology and urban affairs. Specific collections included are the Harris Public Opinion Polls, Yale Human Relations

Area Files, International Survey Library Association, Inter-University Consortium for Political Research, IRSS, Roper Public Opinion Research Center, Southeastern Regional Survey, and U.S. Census Data. Publications include various monographs, indexes, catalogs and bibliographies. Services are available to users inside the organization and, for a fee, outside the Institute for Research in Social Science.

SECTION III

A bibliography of basic governmental, institutional, and organizational documents assembled by the United Nations Conference on the Human Environment, held at Stockholm, Sweden, June 5-16, 1972.

INTRODUCTION

This bibliography is a list of the documents which will be available in the Conference library which is to be set up at Stockholm for consultation by participants in the Conference. The contents of the Conference library, while not being official Conference documents, will include the bulk of the source material from which the Conference documents were drawn.

The bibliography lists the national reports, case studies and other basic documents received by the Conference Secretariat from States invited to the Conference in accordance with General Assembly resolution 2850 (XXVI) and the basic documents received from members of the United Nations system and other sources, including intergovernmental and nongovernmental sources.

It should be noted that the basic documents listed are those which have been specially prepared in connection with the secretariat's preparations for the Conference. When a basic document has been revised, only the revised version is listed. In most cases, these documents have not hitherto been accessible outside the Conference secretariat.

The Conference secretariat has also received numerous background documents which were not specially prepared for the Conference but which have been drawn upon in the preparation of Conference documents. However, papers in the latter category have not been listed in this bibliography. Further information on these background documents may be obtained from the Conference secretariat.

The title of each document and information concerning authorship and date are given in the language of the original provided it is in either English, French or Spanish; if it is not in one of those languages, a translation into one is provided. The abbreviations (E) for English, (F) for French and (S) for Spanish are used to indicate these three languages, in one or the other of which nearly all the documents were submitted.

The entries under each heading of this bibliography are listed according to the English alphabetical order of the source of the document. In the case of basic documents relating to specific subject areas, the principal subject areas in question are indicated by the appropriate Roman numeral.

Subject area (I)	Human settlements
Subject area (II)	Natural resources
Subject area (III)	Pollutants
Subject area (IV)	Educational, informational, social and cultural aspects
Subject area (V)	Development and environment
Subject area (VI)	International organizational implications

It should be noted that a number of topics listed for consideration under one subject area in the report of the Preparatory Committee on its second session (A/CONF.48/PC/9, para. 20) have in fact been treated in the Conference documents on other subject areas. Thus, for example, topic III(c)(iii) — Land, is covered in the recommendations on subject area (II).

In such cases, while the basic documents submitted may refer to the subject area under which the relevant topics were originally located, the annotations in this bibliography refer to the subject areas in which the topics were actually treated.

In cases where the scope of a document is not limited to one or two subject areas, this is indicated by the abbreviation (Gen.), which stands for General. No indication of subject area is given for national reports since, by definition, they cover the whole range of environmental problems.

The basic documents listed in this bibliography comprise 403 documents totaling some 14,750 pages as follows.

From states invited to the Conference	Documents	Pages
National reports	85	4,042
Case studies	35	1,643
Other documents	33	1,185
Total	153	6,870

From United Nations system		
United Nations bodies	42	2,084
Agencies and IAEA	89	1,352
Total	131	3,436

From other sources		
Intergovernmental organizations	17	811
International nongovernmental organizations	57	1,020
National organizations, etc.	33	1,949
Total	107	3,780

Draft position papers	8	596

Other papers	4	70
Grand total	403	14,752

The designations employed and the presentation of material in this document do not imply the expression of any opinion whatsoever on the part of the Secretariat of the United Nations concerning the legal status of any country or territory or of its authorities, or concerning the delimitation of its boundaries.

BASIC DOCUMENTS RECEIVED FROM STATES
INVITED TO THE CONFERENCE

in accordance with General Assembly Resolution 2850 (XXVI)

NATIONAL REPORTS ON ENVIRONMENTAL PROBLEMS

A number of governments have provided the secretariat with draft
or provisional national reports. These reports are included in this
list, on the understanding that the definitive versions will be substi-
tuted for them as soon as they are received.

Afghanistan
Environmental problems of Afghanistan; Kabul University, Kabul;
June 25, 1971; 11 pp. (E)

Algeria
Rapport national; 31 pp. (F)

Argentina
Informe nacional; República Argentina; 1971; 30 pp. (S)

Australia
*Australian national report on problems of the human environ-
ment;* (incl. contribution by National Capital Development Commission); 33 pp. 6 maps (E)

Austria
National report; 66 pp. (E)

Belgium
Monographie de pays sur des problèmes relatifs à l'environment;

Belgium (continued)
Commission interministérielle de la politique scientifique, Services du Premier Ministre; 30 juin 1971 avec Addendum 1 du 1er mars 1972; 38 pp. (F)

Bolivia
Informe nacional de Bolivia sobre el medio humano; Ministerio de Relaciones Exteriores y Culto, Comisión Interministerial Permanente; La Paz, marzo de 1971; 27 pp. (S)

Botswana
National report; Ministry of Agriculture; Gaborone, January 1972; 13 pp. (E)

Brazil
Brazilian national report (preliminary notes); Brasilia, April 1971; 58 pp. (E)

Burma
Problem of human environment; 8 pp. (E)

Burundi
Les problèmes du milieu au Burundi; Bujumbura, fevrier 1972; 9 pp. (F)

Cameroon
Rapport national sur l'environnement; Ministère du plan et de l'aménagement du territoire; 74 pp. (F)

Canada
Canada and the world environment (provisional national report); 49 pp. 2 maps (E)

Central African Republic
Rapport national de la République centrafricaine; 52 pp. (F)

Ceylon
Problems of the human environment; 1971; 31 pp. (E)

Chad
Rapport national de la République du Tchad; 35 pp. (F)

Chile
Informe para la Conferencia de las Naciones Unidas sobre el medio

Chile (continued)
humano; Santiago de Chile, mayo de 1971; 25 pp. (S)

Congo (People's Republic)
Rapport national sur l'environnement; 48 pp. (F)

Cyprus
Report by the Cyprus Council for Nature Conservation; Forest Department, Ministry of Agriculture and Natural Resources; Nicosia, March 1971; 19 pp. (E)

Czechoslovakia
Problems relating to environment; Prague, May 1971; 62 pp. (E)

Denmark
National report on the human environment; 30 pp. (E)

Ecuador
Breve consideración sobre la problemática del medio ambiente humano — caso ecuatoriano; Junta Nacional de Planificación y Coordinación Económica; Quito; 47 pp. (S)

Egypt
National report; October, 1971; 55 pp. (E)

Federal Republic of Germany
National report of the Federal Republic of Germany; Bonn; September 1971; 74 pp. (E)

Finland
Finnish national report; 67 pp. 1 map (E)

France
Rapport francais; P. Randet, Ingénieur géneral, Ponts et Chaussées; 44 pp. (F)

Gabon
Rapport du Gabon; 8 pp. (F)

Ghana
Major problems of the human environment in Ghana; Accra; August 1971; 14 pp. (E)

Greece
A preliminary report on physical environmental problems in Greece;
D. Katochianos, Ministry of Coordination and Centre of Planning
and Economic Research; Athens, March 1971; (incl. addendum);
26 pp. (E)

Guatemala
Informe nacional; Secretaría General del Consejo Nacional de
Planificación Económica; Guatemala, 1 de marzo de 1971; (incl.
addendum); 195 pp. (S)

Haiti
Rapport du Gouvernement Haitien; 15 pp. (F)

Holy See
*Rapport du Saint-Siège en vue de la Conférence sur l'environne-
ment;* 1972; 26 pp. (F)

Hungary
*The national ecological monograph of the Hungarian People's
Republic;* Department for Regional and Town Planning, Ministry
of Building and Urban Development; Budapest, January 1971;
40 pp. (E)

Iceland
National report; 21 pp. (E)

India
National report prepared by the Committee on Human Environment, in 4 volumes: *Some aspects of the environmental degradation and its control in India;* May 1971; 114 pp. (E); *Some aspects of rational management of natural resources;* May 1971;
59 pp. (E); *Some aspects of problem of Human settlements in
India;* May 1971; 72 pp. (E); *Annex: Quantitative projections of
economic and demographic situation 1968-69 to 1985-86;* January
1971; 45 pp. (E)

Indonesia
Environmental problems of Indonesia — a country report; Revised edition; Djakarta, 1972; 23 pp. (E)

Iraq
Problems of environmental pollution; Baghdad, May 31, 1971;
27 pp. (E)

Iran
  Iran national report (including Annex: Scouting in Iran); 69 pp. (E)

Ireland
  National report on problems relating to environment; (Final version);
  May 1971; 44 pp. (E)

Israel
  The environment in Israel; Jerusalem, March 1971; 62 pp. (E)

Italy
  Rapport du Gouvernement Italien; 197 pp. (F)

Ivory Coast
  Projet de rapport national; Abidjan; juillet 1971; 39 pp. (F)

Jamaica
  National report; 36 pp. (E)

Japan
  Problems of the human environment in Japan; March 31, 1971;
  63 pp. (E)

Jordan
  Problems of human environment in Jordan; National Planning
  Council, Amman; 23 pp. (E)

Kenya
  National report on the human environment in Kenya; Working
  Committee for the UN Conference on the human Environment;
  Nairobi, June 1971; 149 pp. (E)

Kuwait
  Human environment — national report; 41 pp. (E)

Luxembourg
  Les problèmes de l'environnement au Grand-Duché de Luxembourg;
  17 pp. (F)

Madagascar
  Rapport national; Tananarive, Mai 1971; 46 pp. (F)

Malawi
  Human environment in Malawi; P.N. Mwanza, University of Malawi,

Malawi (continued)
Blantyre; 20 pp. (E)

Malaysia
Report of the Government of Malaysia; April 1, 1971; 26 pp. (E)

Malta
Country monograph on problems relating to environment; (ECE
doc. ENV/CONF/B. 25, March 3, 1971); 9 pp. (E)

Mexico
Informe nacional; Comisión Preparatoria de la participación de
México en la Conferencia de las Naciones Unidas sobre el Medio
Humano; 90 pp. (S)

Morocco
Projet de rapport national; Premier Ministre, Délégation au Plan et
au Développement Régional; Rabat; décembre 1971; 30 pp. (F)

Nepal
National report on human environment; National Planning Commission Secretariat; Kathmandu, October 19, 1971; 18 pp. (E)

Netherlands
Problems of the human environment in the Netherlands; 88 pp. (E)

New Zealand
New Zealand report; 28 pp. (E)

Niger
Rapport national; Niamey; Juin 1971; 33 pp. (F)

Nigeria
Provisional National report; Federal Ministry of Economic Development and Reconstruction; Lagos, 1971; 40 pp. (E)

Norway
National report; Royal Ministry of Foreign Affairs, Norwegian
National Committee; 54 pp. (E)

Pakistan
*Pakistan country paper on marine pollution, monitoring or sur-
veillance, conservation and soils;* 6 pp. (E)

Peru

Informe sobre el detêrioro del medio ambiente; Ministerio de Salud; 1971; 27 pp. (S)

Philippines

National report of the Republic of the Philippines; Manila, May 1971; 55 pp. (E)

Poland

The protection of the enviroment in Poland; February, 1971; 24 pp. (E)

Portugal

National report to United Nations conference on human environment; Presidencia do Conselho, Junta Nacional de Investigacáo Cientifica e Technologica; 56 pp. (E)

Romania

Rapport sur les problèmes relatifs à l'environnement dans la République socialiste de Roumanie; 37 pp. (F)

Saudi Arabia

A report on the environment in Saudi Arabia; Ministry of Agriculture and Water; September 1971; 13 pp. (E)

Senegal

Rapport à là Conférence des Nations Unies sur l'environnement; Commission Nationale de l'Environnement; 59 pp. (F)

Singapore

Singapore's national report on the environment; Environmental Control Organization, Planning Committee; February 1971; 79 pp. (E)

Spain

Memoria española sobre el medio ambiente; 32 pp. (S)

Sudan

National report on human environment; National Council for Research; Khartoum, March 1971; 49 pp. (E)

Swaziland

National report; 22 pp. (E)

Sweden
National report to UN on the human environment; Stockholm,
1971; 69 pp. (E)

Switzerland
Les problèmes d'environnement en Suisse; 40 pp. (F)

Syria
National report; 36 pp. (Arabic)

Thailand
Environmental problems in Thailand; Committee on Environmental
Quality Control, National Research Council; April 1972; 44 pp. (E)

Togo
Les problèmes de l'environnement au Togo; Présidence de la
République, Ministère des Affaires étrangères; 15 pp. (F)

Tunisia
Rapport national de la Commission sur l'environnement; 1972;
72 pp. (F)

Turkey
*Turkey's national report to the United Nations on the human en-
vironment;* State Planning Organization and Ministry of Reconstruction and Development; Ankara 1972 (incl. corrigendum);
60 pp. (E); Turkey also submitted its country monograph
ENV/CONF/B. 20 of November 11, 1970.

Uganda
National report on the human environment; 98 pp. (E)

Ukrainian Soviet Socialist Republic
*Problems of the human environment and their solution in the
Ukrainian Socialist Republic (Country monograph)* — translation;
19 pp. (E)

United Kingdom
The human environment: the British view; London, H.M.S.O.,
1972; 42 pp. 3 figs. (E)

United States of America
National report on the human environment; 57 pp. (E)

Yugoslavia
National report on the human environment; 25 pp. (E)

Zaire
Problèmes de l'environnement en République démocratique du Congo; This report was submitted before the name of this country was changed. 42 pp. (F)

CASE STUDIES

Australia
Development of the new towns of Canberra; National Capital Development Commission; Canberra, October 1971; (+ appendices); 41 pp. (E) (I)

Pollution of the marine waters of the Bass Strait Region of Tasmania; Division of Environmental Control, Department of Labour and Industry; Hobart, Tasmania, February 1971; 20 pp. (E) (III)

Canada
Mercury crisis in Canada; 31 pp. (E) (III)

Canadian water resource management in the Saint John River Basin; Dept. of the Environment; October 20, 1971; 56 pp. (E) (II)

The conservation of a watershed; W.R. Hanson, Eastern Rockies Forest Conservation Board; Calgary, May 1971 (+ corrigendum); 27 pp. (E) (II)

Conservation in Canada — natural resources and historic sites; Task Force on Conservation of Natural Resources and Historic Sites; Ottawa, May 1971; 208 pp. (E) (II/IV)

Urban Canada — problems and prospects, Le Canada urbainses problèmes et ses perspectives; report prepared by N.H. Lithwick for Minister responsible for Housing; Ottawa, 1970; 236 pp. (E); 262 pp. (F) (I)

An appraisal of social problems and needs in the Haldimand-Norfolk area; C. De'Ath et al, Planning and Resources Institute, University of Waterloo; December 31, 1970; 86 pp. (E) (IV)

The Canada land inventory — objectives, scope and organization;

Canada (continued)
Dept. of Regional Economic Expansion; 55 pp. (E) (II)

A case study of soil erosion by wind in the Palliser Triangle in Central Canada; C.H. Anderson, Swift Current Research Station, Dept. of Agriculture; 26 pp. (E) (II)

Federal Republic of Germany
Industry and Landscape, using the Rhineland brown coal area as an example; G. Olschowy; Bonn – Bad Godesberg; November 1971; 24 pp. (E) (I/II)

Progress of technological and economic development in harmony with environmental protection; 67 pp. (E); 1 vol., including five case studies entitled:

Progressive emission control in trade and industry; 10 pp. (III)

Cooperation between industry and the public authorities, as demonstrated by the example of "Gesellschaft zur Beseitung von Sondermüll in Bayern mbH". (Limited Liability company for the disposal of special refuse in Bavaria); 5 pp. (I)

Water supply associations in the Rhenish-Westphalian industrial area, as examples of cooperation between industry and public authorities; 18 pp. (I)

Regional water-conservation methods as applied in the Bavarian Lake District (circular mains); 17 pp. (I/II)

Reducing the incidence of environmental chemicals, e.g., in the case of plant protection; 15 pp. (II/III)

Finland
The Finnish forest resources and their utilization; A. Haapanen and S. Kellomäki, Dept. of Silviculture, University of Helsinki; 1971; 49 pp. (E) (II)

France
Villes nouvelles et environnement – cas de la ville nouvelle de Vaudreuil; Secrétariat interministériel des villes nouvelles – Mission interministérielle pour l'environnement; mai 1971; 12 pp. (F) (I)

India
Delhi – a case study of a city undergoing planned development;

India (continued)
Planning Commission – Committee on Human Environment; 34 pp. (E) (I)

Iran
The wildlife parks and protected regions of Iran; December 1971; 30 pp. (E) (II/IV)

Italy
Outline of air pollution monitoring and research in Italy; 7 pp. (E) (III)

Japan
Distribution of lead in the air near city roads; Y. Kobayashi et al; 21 pp. (E) (III)

Comprehensive river-basin wide sewerage study, with an example of Lake Biwa Basin; July 1971; 52 pp. (E) (I)

Formulation and implementation of environmental pollution control programs in Japan; July 1971; 51 pp. (E) (III)

Re-development of the Kyoto Area: an approach to natural disaster prevention measures in Japan; October 1971; 22 pp. (E) (I)

Working papers of Japanese participants for a conference on the effects of trace metals on human health (Honolulu; February 1971); 112 pp. (E) (III): *Mechanism of the occurrence of the Minamata disease;* S. Kitamura. *Present status of the nationwide survey of mercury levels in flesh of river fish in Japan;* K. Ueda. *Some plan for future studies for low level of lead in the human being;* K. Horiuchi. *Air pollution by trace metals in Japan;* Y. Kobayashi et al. *Itai-Itai (Ouch-Ouch) disease and cadmium and its health effect in Japan;* I. Shigemutsu et al. *Environmental pollution by cadmium and its health effect in Japan;* K. Tsuchiya. *Absorption and accumulation of cadmium compounds via the oral route;* K. Tsuchiya.

Kenya
Urbanization and environment in Kenya; prepared under the direction of the Working Committee for the UN Conference on the Human Environment; Nairobi; November 1971; 27 pp. (E) (I)

New Zealand
Taupo Basin: a New Zealand study in environmental management;
(incl. map, 5 figs., 16 pp. plates); 52 pp. (E) (Gen.)

Poland
The environment of the central areas of cities: Warsaw; S.
Jankowski, Town Planning Institute of Warsaw, in coopera-
tion with ESA/CHBP; 33 pp. + figures, plates + figures,
(E) (I)

Case studies prepared under the auspices of the Polish Committee
for the Protection of the Environment, Warsaw; 1971: *Polish-
Czechoslovak bilateral cooperation in the area of the water pollution control;* (Paper no. 8); 7 pp. (E) (III). *Polish experience concerning protection of waters against salinity;* A. Symonowicz et al,
August 1971 (Paper no. 9); 18 pp. (E) (II). *Polish experience in
counteracting the negative effects of heated effluents on environment;* St. Kolaczkowski; August 1971 (Paper no. 10); 13 pp. (E)
(III)

Sudan
*Mass resettlement of the population of the lands flooded by the
lands flooded by the Aswan High Dam — a socio-economic appraisal of the resettlement of the people of Wadi Halfa at Khashm el
Girba Agricultural Scheme:* M.Y. Sukkar and M.H. El Jack, National Council for Research; December 1971; 55 pp. (E) (I/II)

Sweden
*Air Pollution across national boundaries: the impact on the environ-
ment of sulfur in air and precipitation;* Swedish Preparatory Committee for the Conference; Stockholm; August 30, 1971; 96 pp.
(E) (III)

Switzerland
La pollution thermique en Suisse; R. Pedroli, Office fédéral de la
protection de l'environnement; Berne, le 28 juin 1971; 19 pp. (F) (III)

The impact of transportation on the environment; E. Basler and
H. Ransen; June 3, 1971; 8 pp. (E) (I)

United Kingdom
*Control of polychlorinated biphenyl pollution in the United King-
dom;* 11 pp. (E) (III)

United States of America
Guidelines for the average citizen; November 1, 1971; 24 pp.
(E) (IV)

Yugoslavia
Problems of development and environmental preservation of the Upper Soca Region; Ljubljana; July 6, 1971; 13 pp. (E) (II)

OTHER BASIC DOCUMENTS

Algeria
Journées nationales d'informations; Comité national intérministériel pour l'environnement; Alger, 23-29 Fevrier 1972; 86 pp. (F) (Gen)

Australia
Proposal for international action on insect viruses; D.F. Waterhouse, Commonwealth Scientific and Industrial Research Organization; Canberra; November 1971; 7 pp. (E) (III)

Canada
Canadian basic paper on "gene pools"; 7 pp. (E) (II)

Czechoslovakia
Education and training in the field of environment; J. Koči, Ministry of Education; Prague; July 9, 1971; 10 pp. (E) (IV)

Federal Republic of Germany
A programme for the protection of the human environment; 134 pp. (E) (Gen.)

France
Rapports préparés par le Ministère de la protection de la nature et de l'environnement — Mission interministérielle pour l'environnement (France):

Les parcs naturels régionaux en France; Paris; mai 1971; 12 pp. (F) (II/IV)

Environnement et action régionale; Paris; juin 1971; 12 pp. (F) (I)

Environnement et développement; Paris; juin 1971; 10 pp. (F) (V)

Iceland
A human environment sensitive to climatic changes; Ministry for Foreign Affairs; 1972; 50 pp. (E) (III)

Italy
Proposals for a global strategy of the environment; 7 pp. (E) (Gen.)

Japan
Air pollution control in Japan; Environment Agency; May 1972; 66 pp. (E) (III)

Pollution related diseases and relief measures in Japan; Environment Agency; May 1972; 34 pp. (E) (III)

Water pollution control in Japan; 57 pp. (E) (II/III)

Madagascar
La conservation des sols et des eaux à Madagascar; Direction des eaux et forêts et de la conservation des sols; mai 1971; 89 pp. (F) (II)

La protection de la nature à Madagascar; juin 1971; 55 pp. (F) (II/IV)

Netherlands
Environmental information and education; Ministry of Cultural Affairs, Recreation and Social Welfare; Rijswijk; October 1970; 30 pp. (E) (IV)

New Zealand
The soil factor in global planning of environmental control, with special reference to the Pacific sector; M. Fieldes, Department of Scientific and Industrial Reserach; 1971; 18 pp. (E) (II)

Peru
El mercurio como contaminante del medio marino; F. Valdez Zamudio, Ministerio de Pesquería; Lima, agosto de 1971; 49 pp. (S) (III)

Poland
Papers prepared under the auspices of the Polish Committee for the Protection of the Environment, Warsaw 1971. Paper no. 1 in this series is the Polish national report.

Physical planning: the tool for improving human environment; B. Malisz (paper no. 2); 13 pp. (E) (I)

Planning of geological research and programming of the exploitation

Poland (continued)
of mineral raw materials; J. Czermiński, Institute of Geology
(paper no. 3); 7 pp. (E) (II)

*Development of mining areas and principles in eliminating negative
effects of exploitation of mineral resources;* B. Krupiński and Z.
Lang; (paper no. 4); August 1971; 20 pp. (E) (II)

Legislative basis for the protection of habitat in Poland; W. Brze-
ziński (paper no. 5); 30 pp. (E) (Gen.)

Standards in protection of the natural environment; I. Ordon,
Polish Standards Committee (paper no. 6); 17 pp. (E) (III)

Protection of marine environment in Poland; August 1971; (paper
no. 7); 12 pp. (E) (III)

Spain
*Defensa de la riqueza forestal — la lucha contra los incendios y
las plagas forestales;* Madrid, mayo de 1971; 58 pp. (S) (II)

Sweden
*The human work environment: Swedish experiences, trends and
future problems;* Swedish Preparatory Committee for the Conference; Stockholm; August 13, 1971; 69 pp. (E) (I/IV)

*Urban conglomerates as psychosocial human stressors: general
aspects, Swedish trends, and psychological and medical implications;* G. Carlestam and L. Levi; prepared for Swedish Preparatory
Committee; 74 pp. (E) (I/IV)

United Kingdom
International surveillance and monitoring of the environment;
May 1971; 7 pp. (E) (III)

International standards for pollution control; 10 pp. (E) (III)

Basic paper on marine pollution; 12 pp. (E) (III)

*The United Kingdom experience in dealing with oil pollution of
the sea;* Department of Trade and Industry et al; 13 pp. (E) (III)

United States of America
Suggestions developed within the US Government for consideration

United States of America (continued)
by the Secretary General of the Conference; Committee on International Environmental Affairs; Department of State publication 8608, Washington; August 10, 1971; 106 pp. (E); 1 vol., including papers entitled:

Conservation of soil resources; 9 pp. (II)

Environmental education and training; 5 pp. (IV)

Genetic pools; 18 pp. (II)

Incorporating environmental considerations in policies and and programs for economic growth; 7 pp. (V)

Information systems for international environmental decisions; 3 pp. (IV)

Limiting the release of pollutants into the environment; 9 pp. (III)

Marine pollution; 13 pp. (III)

Monitoring the global environment; 14 pp. (III)

Research, development and analysis; 15 pp. (Gen.)

World Heritage Trust; 4 pp. (IV)

Zambia
Technical memorandum on ecological upheavals threatening Southern Africa; June 23, 1971; 3 pp. + plates and map; (E) (III)

BASIC DOCUMENTS PREPARED WITHIN
THE UNITED NATIONS SYSTEM

UNITED NATIONS BODIES

As a result of consultations between the interested United Nations departments and agencies and the Conference secretariat, a number of departments and agencies accepted responsibility for preparing basic papers on specific topics listed in paragraph 20 of the report on the second session of the Preparatory Committee (A/CONF. 48/ PC. 9). Departments and agencies other than the one responsible for a particular paper were invited to make contributions to that paper on aspects within their competence. This section of the bibliography lists both basic papers and contributions.

Administrative Committee on Coordination (ACC):

Annex II to the consolidated document on the UN system and the human environment — activities of the UN organizations in relation to the agenda for the Stockholm conference. The consolidated document and Annex I are published as document A/CONF.48/12; 55 pp. (E) (VI)

Division of Human Rights:

Human rights and scientific and technological developments: problems concerning the human environment; 5 pp. (E) (Gen.)

Economic and Social Affairs (ESA)/Centre for Housing, Building and Planning (CHBP). cf. joint paper with ESA/Population Division:

Comprehensive development planning (including annexes);

ESA/CHBP (continued):

May 1971; 77 pp. (E) (I)

Management of settlements development; May 1971; 66 pp. (E) (I)

Rural development; May 1971; 64 pp. (E) (I)

Housing and related facilities; May 1971; 60 pp. (E) (I)

Transitional and marginal areas; May 1971; 56 pp. (E) (I)

Problems of central city areas (including summary); May 1971; 35 pp. (E) (I)

Recreation and leisure; May 1971; 36 pp. (E) (I)

Interaction between building and the environment of human settlements; H. Ramic; May 1971; 30 pp. (E) (I)

Summaries of papers prepared by ESA/CHBP on subject area (I); May 1971; 59 pp. (E) (I)

Proposed actions [from papers prepared by ESA/CHBP on subject area (I)] ; 19 pp. (E) (I)

ESA/Division of Public Finance and Financial Institutions:

Pollution taxes (preliminary report); with R.E. Slitor, U.S. Treasury; May 28, 1971; 133 pp. (E) (III)

Note sur une politique fiscale et financière de lutte contre la pollution à l'échelle national et internationale; Max Cluseau, Professeur à l'Université des Sciences sociales de Toulouse; 91 pp. (F) (III)

ESA/Population Division (in cooperation with CHBP):

Population growth and distribution; May 1971; 54 pp. (E) (I)

ESA/Public Administration Division:

Organizational and administrative aspects of environmental problems at various levels (including abstract); L.K. Caldwell; May 1971; 71 pp. (E)

ESA/Resources and Transport Division (RTD):

Development and environmental aspects of transportation in the context of human settlements; with J.S. Revis, Institute of Public Administration, Washington, D.C., USA; June 1971; 74 pp. (E) (I)

Prospects for the development of less-polluting sources of energy; W.T. Reid, Batelle Institute, USA; June 1971; 67 pp. (E) (II/III)

Energy and environmental policy for developing countries; J.K. Delson; June 1971; 50 pp. (E) (II)

Evaluation of new technologies for the detection, monitoring and analysis of atmospheric pollutants released by energy enterprises; G.L. Rao, Columbia University, New York, USA; June 1971; 48 pages (E) (II/III)

Environmental aspects of mineral resources development — mining operations; T. Falkies, Pennsylvania State University, USA; June 1971; 28 pp. (E) (II/III)

Environmental aspects of mineral resources development — mineral processing; F.A. Aplan, Pennsylvania State University, USA; June 1971; 28 pp. (E) (II/III)

Environmental aspects of transport for natural resources development; with R.E. Rechel and R. Witherspoon, Institute of Public Administration, Washington, D.C., USA; June 1971; 49 pp. (E) (II)

The impact of the motor vehicles on air, noise and safety — problems and policies; with S. Myers, Institute of Public Administration, Washington, D.C., USA; June 1971; 48 pp. (E) (III)

Gas, oil and coal purification from the standpoint of environmental quality control; A.M. Squires, City College, New York, USA; June 1971; 40 pp. (E) (III)

The development of smokeless fuels from coal from the standpoint of minimizing environmental pollution; F.C. Schora and C.W. Matthews, Institute of Gas and Technology, Chicago, USA; June 1971; 34 pp. (E) (III)

Recovery and utilization of waste heat from the standpoint of minimizing pollution; K. Goldsmith; June 1971; 31 pp. (E) (III)

ESA/RTD (continued):

Some aspects of pollution reduction through improved energy conversion and utilization; R.J. Schoeppel, Oklahoma State University, USA; June 1971; 49 pp. (E) (III)

Technological and economic prospects for the development of low-cost smokeless fuels; A. Lahiri, Central Fuel Research Institute, India; June 1971; 65 pp. (E) (III)

Environmental aspects of water resources managements; W.C. Ackermann, President, Committee on Water Research of ICSU; June 1971; 44 pp. (E) (II)

Management of water resources common to more than one national jurisdiction; I.K. Fox et al, University of Wisconsin, USA; June 1971; 43 pp. (E) (II)

Co-operative measures for maintaining and improving the quality of the hydrosphere; E.F. Gloyna et al; June 1971; 68 pp. (E) (II)

Means of preventing or decreasing flood losses; W.R.D. Sewell, University of Victoria, Canada; June 1971; 30 pp. (E) (I)

Means of preventing or minimizing damage from earthquakes; G.V. Berg, University of Michigan, USA; June 1971; 22 pp. (E) (I)

ESA/Social Development Division:

Ethics and the environment; May 19, 1971; 7 pp. (E) (IV)

Office for Inter-Agency Affairs:

Assistance in cases of natural disaster (E/4994) May 13, 1971; 72 pp. (E) also in (F)(R)(S) (I)

United Nations Industrial Development Organization (UNIDO):

Industry in relation to the planning and management of human settlements for environmental quality; 25 pp. (E) (I)

Industrial development and the environment (revised); 54 pp. (E) (V)

Pollutants and nuisances from manufacturing industries (draft – incomplete); 51 pp. (E) (III)

United Nations Institute for Training and Research (UNITAR):

International cooperation for pollution control; D. Serwer; UNITAR Research Report No. 9; New York, February 1972; 76 pp. (E) (III)

Marine pollution problems and remedies, by O. Schachter and D. Serwer; UNITAR Research Report No. 4; New York, November 1970; 52 pp. (E) (III)

United Nations Scientific Committee on Effects of Atomic Radiation (UNSCEAR):

Assessment and control of environmental contamination: experience with artificial radioactivity (revised); G.C. Butler (Canada), I.L. Karol (USSR), B.Lindell (Sweden), D.J. Stevens (Australia) and V. Zeleny (Czechoslovakia); June 28, 1971; 18 pp. (E) (III)

SPECIALIZED AGENCIES AND IAEA

Food and Agriculture Organization of the United Nations (FAO):

The environmental aspects of natural resource management — agriculture and soils; 42 pp. (E) (II)

Forestry; 39 pp. (E) (II)

Fish and fisheries in the context of environmental concern; 15 pp. (E) (II)

Land degradation; 120 pp. (E) (II)

The significance, utilization and conservation of crop genetic resources with Sir O. Frankel; 31 pp. (E) (II)

The environmental aspects of water resources development and management, with suggestions for action; 69 pp. (E) (II)

Pesticides and the environment: the position of FAO; 12 pp. (E) (II/III)

Persistent insecticides in relation to the environment and their unintended effects; L. Ling et al; Rome, May 1972; 52 pp. (E) (II/III).

FAO (continued):

See also FAO Soils Bulletin No. 16, "Effects of intensive fertilizer use on the human environment".

FAO is currently publishing a series of summaries of its basic papers, which will be included in the Conference library.

FAO (jointly with UNESCO and IUCN):

Wildlife, national parks, and recreational resources; 69 pp. (E) (II)

FAO and WHO:

Identification, effects and control of contamination through man's food chain; 43 pp. (E) (III)

Papers prepared by members of the Co-operative Programme of Agro-allied Industries with FAO and other UN organizations; (E). Now available together in a publication entitled "Pesticides in the modern world".

FAO/Industry Co-operative Programme:

Pesticides and the environment; 11 pp. (E) (II/III)

Pesticides in perspective; 4 pp. (E) (II/III)

Fungicides; 7 pp. (E) (II/III)

Herbicides; 6 pp. (E) (II/III)

Organochlorine insecticides; 11 pp. (E) (II/III)

Organophosphorus insecticides; 6 pp. (E) (II/III)

Crop protection and the balance of nature; 6 pp. (II/III)

Integrated control of pests and diseases; 11 pp. (II/III)

The development of a new pesticide; 12 pp. (E) (II/III)

The effect of pesticides on the economy of Latin American countries; 5 pp. (E) (II/V)

The effect of pesticides on the economy of some African countries;

FAO/Industry Co-operative Programme (continued) :

11 pp. (E) (II/V)

The effect of pesticides on the economy of Asian countries; 6 pp. (E) (II/V)

Inter-Governmental Maritime Consultative Organization (IMCO):

Identification and control of pollutants emanating from ships, vessels and other equipment operating in the marine environment (revised February 9, 1972); 36 pp. (E); 43 pp. (F) (III)

International Atomic Energy Agency (IAEA):

The environmental aspects of natural resources management — special problems related to nuclear energy and fossil fuels; 28 pp. (E) (II)

Notes on the IAEA safety standards; 3 pp. (E) (III)

IAEA and WHO:

Identification and control of pollutants and nuisances of broad international significance, with special reference to nuclear activities; 20 pp. (E) (III)

International Civil Aviation Organization (ICAO):

The role of civil aviation in the relationship between technological advancement and the human environment; 11 pp. (E)(F)(S) (I/III)

International Labour Organization (ILO):

Participation of employers' and workers' organizations and other social institutions in activities for the protection of the human environment; 9 pp. (E)

The working environment (environmental specifications for working places); 15 pp. (E) (I)

Educational, informational social and cultural aspects of environmental issues — workers' and management education; 5 pp. (E) (IV)

United Nations Educational, Scientific and Cultural Organization (UNESCO):

The planning and management of human settlements for

UNESCO (continued):

environmental quality — social, cultural and aesthetic factors;
8 pp. (E) (I)

See also joint paper with FAO and IUCN

Effets des interventions de l'homme dans les systèmes écologiques naturels — problèmes écologiques spéciaux aux régions arides, tropicales, arctiques, de marais, insulaires, etc.; 22 pp. (F) (II)

Effects of pollutants and nuisances of international significance: identification and evaluation of related effects on other living organisms and soils; 14 pp. (E) (III)

Effects of pollutants and nuisances of international significance: transport of pollutants in the biosphere; 4 pp. (E) (III)

Identification and study of principal elements in planetary life support system; 17 pp. (E) (II/III)

Educational aspects of environmental issues; 10 pp. (E) (IV)

Social aspects of environment; 9 pp. (E) (IV)

Cultural aspects of the environment; 13 pp. (E) (IV)

Contribution to the report on natural disasters; 15 pp. (E) (I)

Moyens d'introduire la notion d'environnement dans la planification et la gestion d'ensemble de la mise en valeur des ressources naturelles; Note à l'usage du secrétariat de la Conférence des Nations Unies sur l'environnement humain; 5 pp. (F) (II)

The environmental aspects of natural resources management: agriculture and soil; Note for the attention of FAO; 3 pp. (E) (II)

Water; 19 pp. (E) (II)

Cooperative measures for maintaining and improving the quality of the hydrosphere (inland waters); 7 pp. (E) (II)

Genetic pools; 3 pp. (E) (II)

La dégradation des terres; Note à l'attention de la FAO; 7 pp.

UNESCO (continued):

(F) (II)

Management of resources of regional importance; 5 pp. (E) (II)

Informational aspects of environmental issues; 2 pp. (E) (IV)

UNESCO/International Social Science Council:

Environnement: le point de vue des sciences sociales; le 24 mai 1971; 26 pp. (F) (IV)

World Health Organization (WHO). See also joint FAO/WHO paper and joint IAEA/WHO paper:

Water supply, sewage and waste disposal; 41 pp. (E) (I)

Human health and welfare factors; 47 pp. (E) (I)

Contamination through water contact: criteria, guides and standards for permissible levels of human exposure; 69 pp. (E) (III)

Identification and evaluation of the principal acute and long-term effects of environmental agents on man's health, including genetic effects; 52 pp. (E) (III)

Industry in relation to the planning and management of human settlements for environmental quality — climatic, topographic and geological characteristics of particular interest to public health to be taken into account in siting industries; 3 pp. (E) (I)

Housing and related facilities — human requirements; 3 pp. (E) (I)

Transitional and marginal areas; 2 pp. (E) (I)

Recreation and leisure — environmental aspects of tourism; 2 pp. (E) (I)

Transport and communications — air pollution from motor vehicles and other transport systems; 3 pp. (E) (I/III)

Water supply, sewage and waste disposal (recycling); 1 pp. (E) (I)

Hazards from natural disasters — health considerations in natural

WHO (continued):

disasters; 2 pp. (E) (I)

Wildlife and recreational resources — natural resources in relation to recreation and tourism; 2 pp. (E) (II)

Water; 3 pp. (E) (II)

Energy — air pollution from energy production; 3 pp. (E) (II/III)

Minerals — air pollution aspects of mineral resources development; 2 pp. (E) (II/III)

Transport — environmental pollution from pipelines; 1 p. (E) (II/III)

Management of natural resources of special regional importance — water quality in international river basins; 2 pp. (E) (II)

Land — measures required to identify, evaluate and control changes; 7 pp. (E) (II)

Mining — saline water pollution in Poland; 2 pp. (E) (III)

Energy production — air pollutants of public health importance derived from energy production; 4 pp. (E) (III)

Water transport: ocean disposal of sewage from ships in the course of normal operations; 2 pp. (E) (III)

Land transport — effects of pollutants on people; 3 pp. (E) (III)

Industrial pollution — environmental health aspects of chemical and petroleum industry; 2 pp. (E) (III)

Transport of pollutants in the biosphere; contamination through man's food chain, contamination through water supply and air supply, criteria, standards and guides for permissible levels of human exposure; 1 p. (E) (III)

Hydrosphere — health aspects of coastal pollution; 3 pp. (E) (III)

Education — the education of engineers for environmental health; 3 pp. (E) (IV)

WHO (continued):

Environmental considerations in the choice of location of new industries — public health considerations in siting of polluting industries; 2 pp. (E) (V)

WHO/International Agency for Research on Cancer

Working paper; 7 pp. (E) (I/III)

World Meteorological Organization (WMO). A number of the basic papers submitted by WMO have been published by WMO in a slightly different form in "Special Environmental Report No. 2. Selected papers on Meteorology as related to the Human Environment" (WMO, No. 312, Geneva, 1971). This publication will also be available in the Conference library:

Human health and welfare factors; urban climates; 10 pp. (E) (I)

The quality of air as a resource to support life; 15 pp. (E) (II)

Transport of pollutants in the biosphere — contamination through air supply; 16 pp. (E) (III)

Climatic effects of air pollution (Identification and evaluation of air, pollution effects on climate); 27 pp. (E) (III)

Effects of air pollution on materials (Identification and evaluation of effects on goods, materials, buildings, construction, etc.; problems of corrosion); 8 pp. (E) (III)

Control of atmospheric pollution (Atmosphere — measures required to control effects of changes in composition and condition of atmosphere); 19 pp. (E) (III)

Implications of intentional weather and climate modification on the human environment (Atmosphere — measures required to control effects on changes in composition and conditions of atmosphere); M. Neiburger; 22 pp. (E) (III)

Housing and related facilities — building climatology; 13 pp. (E) (I)

Considerations of climatic elements in planning and management of natural resources (environmental considerations in natural resource development); 6 pp. (E) (II)

WMO (continued):

Water — maintenance of water quality; 8 pp. (E) (II)

Regional aspects of air pollution (Management of natural resources of special regional importance); 13 pp. (E) (II)

Identification of principal types of air pollutants, their dispersion and transformation; 10 pp. (E) (II)

Meteorological aspects of transport and monitoring of marine pollution (Hydrosphere); 3 pp. (E) (II)

BASIC DOCUMENTS RECEIVED
FROM OTHER SOURCES

INTERGOVERNMENTAL ORGANIZATIONS (NON-UNITED NATIONS)

African Development Bank:

Environmental Consideration in project appraisal: the experience of the African Development Bank in financing projects in Africa; 8 pp. (E) (V)

Commission of the European Communities:

La place de la Communauté européenne dans l'effort mondial pour la protection et l'amélioration de l'environnement; 51 pp. (F) (Gen.)

Council for Mutual Economic Assistance:

Information on the activities of the Council for Mutual Economic Assistance in the field of the human environment; 10 pp. (Russian) (Gen.)

Council of Europe:

Repercussions of supersonic civil flights on human and natural environment; resolution 512 (1972) adopted by the Consultative Assembly of the Council of Europe on January 25, 1972, with supporting report from Committee on Social and Health Questions; 23 pp. (E)(F) (I/III)

The management of the environment in tomorrow's Europe;

Council of Europe (continued):

proceedings of the European Conservation Conference, Strasbourg, February 9-12, 1970; 255 pp. (E)(F) (Gen.)

Aspects of soil conservation in the different climatic and pedologic regions of Europe; F. Fournier; 158 pp. (E)(F) (II)

Methods for estimating surface water and ground water resources; J. Tricart; 90 pp. (E)(F) (II)

European Nuclear Energy Agency:

Nuclear energy and the environment; May 24, 1971; 11 pp. (E) (II/III)

Inter-American Development Bank:

Environmental problems of agricultural settlement and agrarian reform; H.T. Jorgensen; Washington, D.C.; June 1971; 35 pp. (E) (I)

Conservation and pollution of water resources; H. Olivero, Washington, D.C.; June 8, 1971; 7 pp. (E) (II/III)

Environmental problems of urban development; E. Novaes et al; Washington, D.C.; June 1971; 14 pp. (E) (I)

Accounting for environmental pollution in social cost-benefit analysis of industry; H. Schwartz; Washington, D.C.; June 1971; 7 pp. (E) (III/V)

Organization for Economic Cooperation and Development (OECD):

Problèmes et instruments relatifs à l'allocation des coûts d'environnement; 32 pp. (F); 33 pp. (E) (V)

OECD Development Centre:

Cost-benefit analysis in developed and developing countries (with particular reference to environmental problems): D. Conn; 15 pp. (E) (V)

Rural-urban migration and job location: some thoughts on future research; P.J. Richards; 9 pp. (E) (I)

Organization of American States:

Urbanization and the human environment in Latin America (preliminary version); Division of Urban Development, Dept. of Social Affairs; May 1971; 74 pp. (E) (I)

Development versus environment: an urban systems approach; C. Frankenhoff, University of Puerto Rico; May 1971; 12 pp. (E) (I)

INTERNATIONAL NONGOVERNMENTAL ORGANIZATIONS

Arctic Institute of North America:

Paper addressed to the UN Conference on the Human Environment; Montreal; November 1971; 19 pp. (E) (II/III)

Boy Scouts World Bureau:

Scouting and conservation; Geneva, June 1971; 20 pp. (E) (IV)

Commission of the Churches on International Affairs (World Council of Churches):

Action on the environment and hopes for the future of man — the cruciality of political issues; Geneva, May 24, 1971; 23 pp. (E) (Gen.)

European Institute of Cancerology:

Une charte européenne de prévention des maladies de l'environnement; motion votée par le Symposium cancérologique; Bruxelles, December 2-3, 1971; 2 pp. (F) 2 pp. (E) (I/III)

European Union Against Aircraft Nuisance:

Reduction of aircraft noise nuisance; G. Holmes, UK Federation Against Aircraft Nuisance; May 31, 1971; 3 pp. (E) (I)

Global Atmospheric Research Programme (GARP) (WMO/ICSU):

The role of GARP for environmental problems; statement by Joint Organizing Committee, Stockholm; February 10, 1972; 6 pp. (E) (III)

Groupement international des associations nationales de fabricants de pesticides:

Mémorandums techniques Nos. 1 à 6; 15 pp. (F); 15 pp. (E) (II/III)

ICSU/International Union of Nutritional Sciences:

Proposed position paper for monitoring malnutrition; O.L. Kline, Director, Office of Malnutrition Science Services, Bethesda, Md., USA; 4 pp (E) (I/III)

ICSU/International Union of Pure and Applied Physics (IUPAP):

Draft resolution, submitted by International Commission on Acoustics of IUPAP; 2 pp. (E) (I)

ICSU/Scientific Committee on Problems of the Environment (SCOPE):

Global environmental monitoring; Commission on Monitoring of SCOPE: Stockholm; 1971; 68 pp. (E) (III)

International Air Transport Association (IATA):

IATA statement of policy on noise and atmospheric pollution arising from the operation of aircraft; resolution of IATA Annual General Meeting; Honolulu, November 1971; 3 pp. (E) (I/III)

International Association for Pollution Control:

The focus of worldwide environmental education of the future: J. Pavoni, et al; 23 pp. (E) (IV)

Urban noise; D.J. Hagerty et al; 12 pp. (E) (I)

International Association for the protection of Industrial Property:

The menace to our environment and the protection of industrial property; R.E. Blum; 21 pp. (E) (II)

International Association of Democratic Lawyers:

Declaration sur l'environnement; 6 pp. (F) (Gen.)

International Astronautical Federation:

10 papers selected from the 22nd International Astronautical Congress (Brussels, September 20-25, 1971) for contribution to the Conference on the Human Environment; selected by L. Jaffe and

International Astronautical Federation (continued):

K. Kondratyev; one volume including the following papers: (III)

Numerical experiments on laser sounding of the atmosphere from outer space; V.E. Zuev et al (revised); 20 pp. (E)

The dust-sand flows and storms in the atmosphere from space imagery; B.V. Vinogradov et al (revised); 13 pp. (E)

Meteorological aspects of atmospheric pollution and possibilities of observations from space; K. Kondratyev et al (revised); 33 pp. (E)

Man-made environment as viewed from space: water and air pollution; B.V. Vinogradov (revised); 16 pp. (E)

An application of a space technique for pollution detection; J.J. Hall; 23 pp. (E)

Remote sensing of chlorophyll and temperature in marine and fresh waters; J.C. Arvesen, J.P. Millard; 31 pp. (E)

Environmental quality indices from remote sensing data; W.O. Davis; 14 pp. (E)

Determination and registration of geothermic processes in the range of volcanic activity by satellite air pictures; H. Kaminski; 40 pp. (E)

Global monitoring and remote sensing from satellites; B. Lundholm; 12 pp. (E)

Global survey of atmospheric trace and pollutant molecules; R.A. Toth, C.B. Farmer; 14 pp. (E)

International Building Council:

Conception et organisation du développement des établissements; 15 pp. (F); 14 pp. (E) (I)

International Chamber of Commerce (ICC):

Technology and society: a challenge to private enterprise: background document; 20 pp. (E)(F) (Gen.)

Technology and society: a challenge to private enterprise: statements and conclusions of the 1971 Congress of ICC; 36 pp. (E) (F) (Gen.)

Industry and the environment; 35 pp. (E)(F) (V)

International Commission on Radiological Protection (ICRP):

The role and experience of ICRP in radiation protection; C.G. Stewart and F.D. Sowby; May 17, 1971; 10 pp. (E) (III)

International Confederation of Free Trade Unions (International Housing Committee):

The challenge of the environment; 39 pp. (E)(F)(S)(Gen.)

International Conference of Women Engineers and Scientists:

Contribution of women engineers and scientists to explore the possibilities of eliminating the impairing of the human environment; (including resolution of Third International Conference of Women Engineers and Scientists, Turin); September 5-12, 1971; 10 pp. (E) (Gen.)

International Co-operative Alliance:

Co-operatives and the environment; 6 pp. (E) (IV)

International Council of Monuments and Sites:

Document de base; R.M. Lemaire, Secrétaire général; Louvain, May 27, 1971; 8 pp. (F) (IV)

International Council of Scientific Unions (ICSU) International Biological Programme:

Basic paper; E.B. Worthington, Scientific Director; (including annex, "Plant genetic pools", by O.H. Frankel); May 28, 1971; 12 pp. (E) (II)

International Federation for Housing and Planning:

Conclusions on environmental problems accepted by the General Council; 32nd Congress; Belgrade, June 11, 1971; 2 pp. (E) (I)

International Federation of Landscape Architects:

The problems of human environment; 4 pp. (E) (I/IV)

International Geographical Union/Commission on Man and Environment:

International response to environmental hazards; G.F. White; May 1971; 5 pp. (E) (Gen.)

International Geographical Union/Commission on Man and Environment (continued):

Environmental protection and water development; G.F. White; May 1971; 14 pp. (E) (II)

International Organization of Consumers Unions:

The consumer and the environment; The Hague; May 13, 1971; 4 pp. (E) (IV)

Report on noise; The Hague; 1971; 77 pp. (E) (I)

Position papers submitted to the UN Conference on the Human Environment:

Air pollution caused by motor vehicles; 6 pp. (E) (III)

Solid waste; 2 pp. (E) (I)

Marine pollution; 2 pp. (E) (III)

Education and information; 3 pp. (E) (IV)

International Planned Parenthood Federation:

Population and environment; London; May 25, 1971; 3 pp. (E) (I)

International Road Federation:

Miscellaneous papers (I), including:

Aspects of the design of urban highways; P. Anm; 5 pp. (E)

L'environnement du conducteur; R. Coquand; 3 pp. (F)

The automobile and clean air in the United States; T.C. Mann; 4 pp. (E)

Mobility and environment in Newcastle-upon-Tyne; D.T. Bradshaw and K.A. Galley; 7 pp. (E)

The southwest corridor — a joint development study; L.F. De Marsh; 3 pp. (E)

Urban road planning and the environment; Lord Holford 7 pp. (E)

International Society for Rehabilitation of the Disabled:

Human settlements and the needs of the aged and physically

International Society for Rehabilitation of the Disabled (continued):

handicapped; New York; May 25, 1971; 4 pp. (E) (I)

Remarks; 3 pp. (E) (I)

International Society for Research on Civilization Diseases and Vital Substances:

Human ecological aspects and research of the environment; H.A. Schweigart, President; 21 pp. (E) (Gen.)

International Society of Soil Science:

Environmental aspects of soil management and agricultural practices; F.A. van Baren; 6 pp. (E) (II)

International Touring Alliance:

Prise de position de l'AIT et de ses clubs sur l'environnement en relation avec les loisirs et le tourisme; le 14 avril 1971; 5 pp. (F); 4 pp. (E) (I)

International Union of Building Societies and Savings Associations:

Housing and the Human environment; A.W. Moir; Sydney, Australia; June 28, 1971; 9 pp. (E) (I)

Resolution on the human environment adopted by the Twelth World Congress of the International Union of Building Societies and Savings Associations; Berlin; September 17, 1971; 1 pp(E) (I)

International Union Of Geodesy and Geophysics:

Resolution 20 of XVth General Assembly; Moscow, August 1971; 1 p. (E)(F) (Gen.)

International Union of Local Authorities:

Local government and the human environment; 7 pp. (E) (Gen.)

International Union of Official Travel Organizations (IUOTO):

Resolution XXII/II — questions relating to the human environment; adopted by the XXIInd General Assembly of IUOTO; Ankara, October 1971; 1 p. (E)(F)(S) (I)

International Union of Producers and Distributors of Electrical Energy:

The electricity supply to industry in relation to the environment; March 1, 1972; 13 pp. (E); 14 pp. (F) (II/III)

International Youth Forum for European Conservation Year:

Declaration; Lüneburger Heide; July 25, 1970; 4 pp. (E) (IV)

Union of International Associations:

Communication; Brussels; May 21, 1971; 4 pp. (E) (Gen.)

United Towns Organization:

In favour of a world environment policy; A. Chaudières; 17 pp. (E) (I)

Women's International League for Peace and Freedom:

Statement; 6 pp. (E) (III)

World Association of World Federalists:

A United Nations environment agency; Ottawa; May 26, 1971; 5 pp. (E) (VI)

Stockholm and beyond — a consensus of views expressed by participants to the Windsor Castle Conference on the Human Environment; March 6-9, 1972; 4 pp. (E) (VI)

World Energy Conference:

Environmental conservation and the energy producing industries; 63 pp. (E) (II/III)

World Federation for Culture Collections:

Conservation of genetic pools of micro-organisms; S.M. Martin; Ottawa, May 1971; 20 pp. (E) (II)

World Packaging Organization:

Solid waste — the third pollution; 7 pp. (E) (I)

International project for package disposability factor rating; July 1971; 7 pp. (E) (I)

World Society for Ekistics:

Report from the international conference on education in ekistics; Athens; July 9-10, 1971; 13 pp. (E) (I/IV)

OTHER SOURCES – NATIONAL ORGANIZATIONS, UNIVERSITIES, INDIVIDUALS

It should be noted that most national-level contributions to the preparations for the Conference were made by the organizations and individuals concerned to their national governments.

R. Abbou (France):

Conséquences des pollutions et des nuisances sur la santé publique; 15 pp. (F) (III)

Airport Associations Coordinating Council (USA):

Airports and the human environment; 10 pp. (E) (I)

Albuquerque Department of Environmental Health:

Air pollution problems in Albuquerque (case study); 14 pp. (E) (III)

H. Alfvén (Sweden):

Energy and environment; January 1972; 11 pp. (E) (II)

The American University (Washington, D.C.):

Comprehensive environmental education: a means for inclusion of environmental and ecological principles in university education; Dr. Martha C. Sager, Director, Institute for Environmental Systems Analysis and Management; 26 pp. (E) (IV)

Association des éclaireuses et éclaireurs de France (France):

L'homme et son milieu (Résumé des principales actions menées par les Eclaireuses et éclaireurs de France en 1970); 3 pp. (F) (IV)

Association of Attenders and Alumni of the Hague Academy of International Law:

Annuaire – Communications du XXIIIe Congrès de l'A.A.A., sur le thème "Le droit international de l'environnement humain"; Rabat, Maroc.; 17-22 mai 1972; 160 pp. (F)(E)(Arabic) (Gen.)

J.R. Bellerby et al (UK):

Human ecology and human values; 25 pp. (E) (IV)

Brentree Environmental Center (Milford, Pa., USA):

People and their environment — a case study of curriculum development for conservation education in the United States, 1964-1972; M.J. Brennan, Director; 22 pp. (E) (IV)

J.I. Bregman and S. Megregian (USA):

Water quality standards; 13 pp. (E) (II/III)

S. Chandrasekhar (India):

Demography, development and ecology — India, a case study; 18 pp. (E) (I)

Commission to Study the Organization of Peace (USA):

The United Nations and the human environment; New York, April 1972; 75 pp. (E) (Gen.)

M. Cossa and F. Silvia (USA):

Proposal: A model world environmental education program; January 1972; 30 pp. (E) (IV)

A.J. Drapeau (Canada):

Répertoire international des films sur les sciences de l'eau; Ecole Polytechnique de Montréal, 1972; 98 pp. (F) (II/III)

Forum International, International Ecosystems University, Berkeley, Cal., USA:

The international ecosystems university — a presentation of background materials; 37 pp. (E) (IV)

J.H.N. Garland (UK):

The influence of pollution on the condition of water in the River Trent system; 22 pp. (E) (II/III)

Harlemse Aktiegroep voor International Samenworking (Netherlands):

Petition; 8 pp. (E) (Gen.)

Institute for the Study of International Organizations, University of Sussex (UK):

The United Nations system and the human environment by

Institute for the Study of International Organizations (continued):

B. Johnson, 1971 (ISIO Monograph, first series, number five); 54 pp. (E) (VI)

Institute of Ecology (USA):

Man in the living environment; 273 pp. (E) (Gen.)

The Institute on Man and Science and the Aspen Institute for Humanistic Studies (USA):

International organizations and the human environment, proceedings of a Conference held in May 1971 in Rensselaerville, N.Y.; 44 pp. (E) (VI)

International Institute for Environmental Affairs (New York, USA):

The human environment: science and international decision-making [based on the International Environmental Workshop, Aspen, Colorado (USA), June 20, August 6, 1971, co-sponsored with The Aspen Institute for Humanistic Studies]; 32 pp. (E) (VI)

T.A. Margerison (UK):

The role of public information in environmental policy; 37 pp. (E) (IV)

Massachusetts Institute of Technology (MIT) (USA):

Inadvertent climate modification: Report of the Study of Man's Impact on Climate (SMIC); sponsored by MIT and hosted by the Royal Swedish Academy of Sciences and the Royal Swedish Academy of Engineering Sciences; July 1971; 329 pp. (E) (III)

Man's impact on the global environment, assessment and recommendations for action; Report of the Study of Critical Environmental Problems (SCEP): sponsored by MIT; July 1970; 314 pp. (E) (Gen.)

National Parks and Conservation Association (USA):

Permanent institutions within the United Nations for the protection of the human environment — a preliminary proposal; 12 pp. (E) (VI)

National Pure Water Association (UK):

Prevention of water pollution; May 1971; 6 pp. (E) (II/III)

Smithsonian Institute (Washington, D.C., USA):

The establishment of an international environmental monitoring program — a plan for action; R. Citron, Office of Environmental Sciences; May 1971; 75 pp. (E) (III)

Outline for a feasibility study for the establishment of an international natural disaster warning system; R. Citron; July 1971; 43 pp. (E) (I)

The Stanley Foundation (USA):

Environmental management in the seventies — The Sixth Conference on the United Nations of the Next Decade; Sinaia, Romania, June 1971; 24 pp. (E) (VI)

University of Wisconsin — Green Bay (USA):

Educational aspects of environmental issues; E.W. Weidner, Chancellor (incl. bibliographical note by J.E. Zipperer); 27 pp. (E) (IV)

Environmental education at the University of Wisconsin — Green Bay: a case study; E.W. Weidner, Chancellor; May 1971; 29 pp. (E) (IV)

E. Weissman:

World cities in the future — shelter systems for the future; 11 pp. (E) (I)

E. Wenk, University of Washington (USA):

International institutions for rational management of ocean space; December 6, 1971; 52 pp. (E) (III/IV)

DRAFT POSITION PAPERS

These draft position papers were prepared by consultants on the basis of basic documents received by the Conference secretariat. These papers constituted major inputs to the official Conference documents on subject areas I — VI. It will be recalled that it was at one time planned to publish a position paper on each subject area separately from the action paper on each area but that it was later decided to combine the two concepts and to have only one document for each subject area.

R.N. Gardner:

The international organizational implication of action proposals — first draft; July 5, 1971; 34 pp. (E) (VI)

C. Garnier:

Dimensions socio-culturelles des politiques de l'environement; août 1971; 70 pp. (F) (IV)

B.D.G. Johnson:

The international organizational implications of action proposals — third draft; November 26, 1971; 69 pp. (E) (VI)

P. Johnson-Marshall:

Planning and management of human settlements for environmental quality; Edinburgh 1971; 131 pp. (E) (I)

J. Ludwigson:

Environmental aspects of natural resource management — second draft; Washington, D.C., October 1971; 103 pp. (E) (II)

N. Moore:

Identification and control of pollutants and nuisances; 71 pp. + 1 fig. (E) (III)

G. Oldham:

The environmental aspects of natural resources management — first draft; 78 pp. (E) (II)

D. Wightman:

The international organizational implications of action proposals — second draft; 39 pp. (E) (VI)

OTHER PAPERS

German Democratic Republic
  Problems relating to environment; Berlin, February 1971; 41 pp.
  (E); 46 pp. (Russian); 42 pp. (German)

  *Governmental measures in the GDR to keep waters clean and to
  rationally use ground and surface waters;* 10 pp. (E) (II)

  *The planned development of the environment in the GDR on the
  basis of master plans of the counties;* 9 pp. (E) (I)

  The reclamation of mining areas in the GDR; 10 pp. (E) (II)